I Love Alberta Beef

Alberta Beef
Producers

National Library of Canada Cataloguing in Publication Data

I love Alberta beef / the Alberta Beef Producers.
Includes index.
ISBN 1-894898-19-2
1. Cookery (Beef) I. Alberta Beef Producers.
TX749.5.B43I46 2004   641.6'62   C2004-901783-7

Thanks to the Beef Information Centre for supplying all the recipes and photographs. For more information go to www.beefinfo.org and www.albertabeef.org.

TouchWood Editions acknowledges the financial support for its publishing program from the Government of Canada through the Book Publishing Industry Development Program (BPIDP), the Canada Council for the Arts and the Province of British Columbia through the British Columbia Arts Council

TouchWood Editions Ltd.
Victoria, BC, Canada
www.touchwoodeditions.com
Distributed by:
Heritage House Publishing Ltd.
#108-17665-66A Avenue
Surrey, BC, Canada V3S 2A7
greatbooks@heritagehouse.ca
www.heritagehouse.ca

Printed in Canada

BRITISH
COLUMBIA
ARTS COUNCIL
We acknowledge the support of the Province of British Columbia
through the British Columbia Arts Council

Contents

The Alberta Beef Producers / 4
Buying and Cooking Beef / 8
The Nutritional Benefits of Beef / 16

Recipes
Cooked Beef, Salads and Soups / 18
Ground Beef / 37
Quick Serve Beef / 55
Roasts / 65
Steaks / 88
Stewing Beef / 131

Index / 141

The Alberta Beef Producers

The more than 30,000 beef cattle producers who are stewards of the industry in this province have one organization that represents their collective interests: the Alberta Beef Producers. Run by producers for producers, the Alberta Beef Producers is dedicated to maintaining a truly sustainable, competitive industry.

The Alberta Beef Producers was established in 1969 at the request of five widely diverse farm groups: the Alberta Cattle Breeders Association, the Alberta Dairymen's Association, the Alberta Federation of Agriculture, the Farmers Union of Alberta and the Western Stock Growers' Association.

The ABP is committed to providing leadership to the Canadian beef industry. Through direct support of the Canadian Cattlemen's Association, the Beef Information Centre and the Canada Beef Export Federation, the ABP supports a broad base of programs and policies to ensure Canada's beef industry remains globally competitive.

The Alberta Beef Industry

Alberta's beef industry grew from enterprise and innovation. The first settlers in the late 1800s quickly discovered that Alberta range, farmland and climate were an ideal combination for raising cattle. Today, that innovative spirit coupled with a willingness to adapt new technology has made Alberta the nation's major cattle-producing region and a gateway to world markets for the Canadian beef industry. Alberta cattle producers are committed to ensuring that their industry makes a positive contribution to the economy in a way that is compatible with the sustained and safe use of the land, water and other resources they employ.

Nearly 70 percent of Canada's beef is produced in this province. The largest cattle-feeding network and the largest beef processors are located here, and beef is Alberta's number one agricultural commodity. That translates into significant economic benefits for not only rural areas but the entire Alberta community.

What makes Alberta beef special? A major reason is the way the beef is finished with grain. Alberta beef is famous for its flavour, texture and quality, and grain is certainly part of the equation. Research has shown that consumers prefer tender, juicy beef with the firm, white fat cover of grain-fed cattle.

Beef Industry Commitment to Quality

The beef industry understands the importance of proper animal care and nutrition. For producers, animal care, nutrition and humane handling simply make good business sense because healthy animals that are properly cared for are the most productive and efficient. Producers also recognize animal care, food safety and environmental issues are important to consumers and to society in general. That's why the Alberta Beef Producers is a partner in a national beef quality assurance program that establishes and endorses production standards in these important areas.

Animal Care: The Alberta Beef Producers is taking a leadership role in supporting programs to ensure animals are properly cared for during production and processing. Policies and education programs have been developed to ensure these standards are met. The Alberta Beef Producers works closely with Alberta Farm Animal Care (AFAC), a coalition of industry associations dedicated to establishing programs and policies of animal care in the province.

Food Safety: The Canadian meat inspection process is among the most stringent in the world. Federal inspection is conducted by the Canadian Food Inspection Agency. The Alberta Beef Producers supports meat quality control programs based on internationally recognized Hazard Analysis Critical Control Points (HACCP). Implemented by meat processors, this program ensures beef meets the quality and safety requirements for consumers by preventing biological, chemical or physical contamination of beef throughout the processing chain.

Canadian processing plants have readily adapted HACCP systems in their operations. To ensure Canada's high standards are met, during the meat inspection process trained inspectors with the Canadian Food Inspection Agency (CFIA) carefully examine the animals.

This careful attention to food safety is one of the reasons why Canada has earned a global reputation for ensuring the food that reaches consumers is safe and wholesome.

Nutrition: Today's beef is good for consumers. For example, research shows that, on average, beef is 50 percent leaner than it was 20 years ago. Lean beef is an outstanding nutritional source, supplying 12 essential nutrients, including protein, niacin, vitamins B6 and B12, phosphorus and zinc. Vitamin B12 is important in the production of DNA and the metabolism of all cells. Although many foods are fortified with Vitamin B12, the form found in beef is the most readily usable by the body.

Beef is also an important source of riboflavin, magnesium, potassium and iron. The absorbable iron found in beef contains a high percentage of "heme" iron — a type of iron that is more easily absorbed by the body than the iron found in plant foods such as grains, fruits, and vegetables. Iron deficiency is a common nutrient deficiency, especially among young children, adolescent girls and women of childbearing age.

The Beef Production Chain

Cow/calf operations are the starting point for commercial beef production. There are 2.2 million breeding beef cows and heifers in Alberta, 41 percent of the Canadian total. Cow/calf production is based on an annual schedule, with mother cows usually producing one calf per year. Heifers typically produce their first calf at two years of age.

Mother cows and calves graze pasture during the spring, summer and fall. In typical operations, calves are weaned from their mothers in the fall, from September to November, when they reach a weight of about 160–295 kilograms.

Since cow/calf producer income is based on selling calves, successful cow/calf production depends heavily on animals receiving proper care and nutrition. Producers ensure their breeding females are maintained on a nutritional program with enough nutrients for the mother cow to give birth to a strong, healthy calf, supply milk to the calf and be in condition to rebreed about 80–85 days after calving.

Backgrounding: At least half of the weaned calves produced in Alberta each year are "backgrounded" before they are placed on a feedlot finishing program. Backgrounding is the process of feeding younger, weaned calves a high forage diet, usually lower-cost and more efficient growing rations, either in a feedlot or on pasture to increase their weight to about 341 kilograms. Once these cattle reach the desired weight, they move to the finishing phase.

Feedlot Finishing: Historically, cattle were finished in small farm feedlots. Today, highly specialized cattle feedlots feed most of the province's cattle to market weight. Alberta's natural resources and climate are especially suitable to the cattle feeding industry. There are now 4,000 feedlots in Alberta, making the province the fifth largest cattle feeding area in North America.

As an indication of the high quality of beef produced in Alberta, over 90 percent of animals produced in Alberta feedlots achieve a grade of Canada A, AA, AAA or Prime, the most desired categories within the Canadian meat grading system.

Beef Processing: Alberta is home to Canada's three largest beef processors — modern, efficient processing plants with capacity to process more than 34,000 head of cattle per week. Alberta federal- and provincial-inspected plants processed 2.1 million head of cattle, appproximately 68 percent of the Canadian total in 2003. Alberta has increased its share of the total Canadian beef processing industry from 40 percent in 1984 to 70 percent today.

The sophistication and capacity of beef processing operations has made Alberta a gateway to world markets for the Canadian beef industry. Working with producers and the entire beef chain, the processing industry is leading the way in the development of new products and markets.

Environmental Stewardship

Alberta's cattle industry is committed to producing beef in an environmentally sustainable manner. Through the Alberta Beef Producers policy development, programs and educational efforts are constantly enhanced to uphold this vision. They also formally recognize beef producers who have incorporated environmental protection into their management strategies.

Buying and Cooking Beef

Buying Beef: It is most important to choose the right cut for the cooking method that you want to use. For example, grilled on the barbecue as a kabob, stewing beef cubes may not be very tender, but slowly simmered in a savoury blend of broth and red wine makes stewing beef tender and flavourful. This step-by-step guide will help you to enjoy beef at its best.

What is Aging?: Aging can dramatically improve beef tenderness and flavour. In the aging process, beef is held at controlled temperatures and humidity for a period of time. During this time, enzymes naturally occurring in the meat break down some of the connective tissue that contributes to toughness. For enhanced eating quality, look for beef that is aged at least 10 to 14 days. Check with your meat counter representatives for details about the aging policy of the beef they sell.

✓ Beef cannot be safely aged in a home refrigerator.

What is Marbling and Grading?: Marbling can enhance the juiciness and flavour of beef. It refers to the amount of fine white flecks of fat that you see running through the lean meat. Beef grading can indicate the amount of marbling in the meat. Grading is a voluntary process of the Canadian beef industry. (Grading has nothing to do with inspection, and beef can be sold ungraded.) Canada's top grades, ranging from most to least marbling, are: Canada Prime (available mainly in restaurants), Canada AAA, Canada AA or Canada A.

Why are there Colour Differences in Beef?: Colour can vary due to many factors including packaging material, amount of aging, meat storage temperature and condition of meat. A bright red colour is not always the best indication of freshness or quality. As beef is exposed to oxygen, it quickly turns cherry red. Meat not exposed to oxygen will remain dark. This is why package of ground beef can be red at the surface but dark purple in the center. Likewise, beef in airtight packaging can naturally be a dark purplish colour even on the surface. Beef that has been well aged can have a slightly darker colour. Check the "packaged on" or "best before" date on the label for the best indicator of freshness.

✓ Government regulations prohibit the addition of any colourings, additives or preservatives to fresh beef.

Cooking Methods

Premium Oven Roasts
1. Place roast, fat side up, on rack in roasting pan without lid.
2. Season to taste.
3. Insert meat thermometer into center of roast, avoiding fat or bone. Roast at 325°F (160°C) to the desired internal temperature.
4. Tent with foil for 10–15 minutes to allow the temperature to rise 5°F (3°C).

Oven Roasts
1. Add water to roasting pan to a depth of ½ inch (1.2 cm). Place 2–5 lb. (1–2.4 kg) roast, fat side up, on a rack over water in pan. Do not add extra fat.
2. Season roast to taste and insert meat thermometer into center of roast, avoiding fat or bone.
3. Place uncovered roast in preheated 500°F (260°C) oven. Don't open oven door. After 30 minutes, reduce oven temperature to 275°F (140°C). Cook an additional 1¼ to 1¾ hours for medium doneness (for example, an internal temperature of 160°F/70°C).
4. Remove roast to cutting board. Tent with foil for 10–15 minutes to allow temperature to rise 5°F (3°C). Cut into thin slices across the grain.

✓ Slice only enough roast beef for the meal. Unsliced roast beef does not dry out in the refrigerator as quickly as sliced.

Pot Roasts
1. Season roast. Brown in lightly oiled stockpot or Dutch oven over medium-high heat.

2. Add 1–2 cups (250–500 ml) liquid, such as red wine, broth, canned tomatoes or soup.
3. Simmer, covered, on stovetop or in 325°F (160°C) oven at least 3 hours or until tender. Add chunks of vegetables for final 30 minutes, if desired.

✓ Roasts and steaks cooked to rare or medium-rare doneness are safe to eat. Any bacteria that is on the raw meat exists only on the surface and is eliminated once well cooked.
✓ Indirect heat grilling turns your barbecue into an outdoor oven and is perfect for all types of roasts. Place roast on grill over drip pan on one side of barbeque. Turn heat off just under the roast and cook as directed.
✓ With proper preparation, all beef can be barbecued regardless of the cut.

Doneness Guide for Roasts

Doneness	Rotisserie min./lb	Rotisserie min./kg	Internal Temperature	Indirect Heat Grilling min./lb	Indirect Heat Grilling min./kg
Rare	18–20	40–45	135°F (57°C)	15–20	35–45
Medium	22–25	50–55	155°F (68°C)	25–30	55–65

Stewing Beef
1. Cut meat from bone into cubes, if necessary. Coat beef pieces with a mixture of flour, salt and pepper. In lightly oiled Dutch oven or stockpot, brown meat in batches. Add onions and other seasonings as desired.
2. Add enough liquid, such as broth, tomato juice or red wine, to just cover beef.
3. Simmer, covered, on stovetop or in 325°F (160°C) oven at least 1 hour. Add chunks of vegetables and cook 30 minutes longer.

Grilling Steaks
1. Season with pepper, but do not salt.
2. Grill, broil or pan-fry using medium-high heat, turning only once or twice with tongs.
3. Cook as follows (based on minutes per side):

Marinating Steaks
1. Pierce steak numerous times with fork.
2. Marinate in 1 cup (250 mL) acidic liquid (citrus juice, wine, etc.) plus seasonings for 12–24 hours in refrigerator, or 20–30 minutes if using packaged quick marinades.
3. Grill, broil or pan-fry, turning only once or twice with tongs. Do not cook past medium.

Doneness Guide for Steaks

Thickness	*Minutes per Side*		
	Rare	*Medium*	*Well*
½"–¾" (1–2 cm)	3–4	4–5	5–6
1" (2.5 cm)	4–6	6–7	7–9
1½" (3.5 cm)	8–10	10–14	15–18
2" (5 cm)	10–14	14–18	18–22

✓ Never place cooked meat on the same plate that held raw meat without first washing the plate with hot, soapy water.

The Magic of Marinades

Marinating is an easy way to add delicious flavour to beef and can, at the same time, make less expensive cuts more tender. With so many options at the meat counter, it's great to know that any beef you buy can be barbecued with delicious results!

It takes time to tenderize. The larger the piece of meat or the less tender it is, the longer the marinating time. For example, grilling steaks and premium roasts need to be marinated just for flavour. Beef cut from the chuck, round, flank and skirt will benefit from a marinade's tenderizing ingredients and longer marinating time.

1. Pierce beef all over with fork.
2. Place in sealable freezer bag with your favourite marinade. Use ½ cup (125 ml) marinade per 1 pound (500 g) meat. Add beef and marinate in the fridge (see Marinating Guide for times). Discard marinade.
3. Barbecue steaks or roasts using medium-high heat according to Doneness Guide. When beef is done, remove from grill and tent with foil; let sit 5 minutes (for steaks) or 10–15 minutes (for roasts). Slice meat thinly across the grain to serve.

Marinating Guide

Beef Cuts	Marinating Times
Grilling steaks and premium oven roasts (such as prime rub, top sirloin and rib)	30 minutes to 2 hours
Oven roasts and pot roasts, marinating and simmering steaks (such as round, sirloin tip, cross rib and blade)	12 to 24 hours (larger roasts may take up to 48 hours
Marinating strips and cubes	30 minutes to 1 hour

✓ Try marinating in sealable freezer bags. Mix marinade ingredients right in the bag, add meat, squeeze out the air, and refrigerate. There is no need to turn the meat while marinating, and cleanup is easy!

✓ When you buy beef for marinating, buy extra and freeze some with the marinade. The meat will marinate as it freezes and will marinate still more as it thaws.

✓ Most marinated cuts are best enjoyed cooked just to medium. Grilling steaks and premium oven roasts can be cooked to well done if desired.

✓ Always marinate in the fridge (never at room temperature).

✓ Discard marinade that has been in contact with uncooked meat, or to use as a basting or dipping sauce: plan ahead and reserve a portion before adding to meat. Or bring marinade that has been in contact with uncooked meat to a full rolling boil for at least 1 minute.

Ground Beef

Ground beef is Canada's most popular meat, and is it any wonder? It's a family favourite, quick and easy to prepare, and good for you, too! Ground beef is the great "kitchen chameleon" — use it in stir-fries, casseroles, soups and sauces, or shape it into meatballs, meatloaf or burgers. Dressed up for guests or dressed down for simplicity, ground beef is the perfect starter for so many different recipes!

What's in a name? The label name on a package of raw ground beef refers to its maximum fat content, as regulated by law. In addition, you may find ground beef labeled with the name of the beef cut used for making the grind (such as ground round, ground sirloin, and ground chuck). What to buy? With so many ground beef varieties to choose from, which one do you pick?

Ground Beef Guide

Raw gound beef Label name	Maximum fat content	Best use
Extra Lean, extra lean ground round, extra lean ground sirloin	10%	Cabbage rolls, meatloaf, stuffed peppers and casseroles
Lean, lean ground chuck	17%	All-purpose — flavourful lean burgers, meatballs and chili
Medium	23%	Burgers and meatballs
Regular	30%	Brown and drain for pasta sauce, casseroles and tacos

The label descriptions extra lean, lean, medium or regular refer to the maximum fat levels allowed for all raw ground meats (beef, pork, chicken, turkey, veal and lamb). Recent studies show that all types of ground beef have considerably less fat than the maximums allowed. Cooking reduces the amount of fat on average by one-third, since fat drips out when barbecuing or broiling and can be drained off after pan-frying.

Simply Cooked Ground Beef
1. Cook ground beef in non-stick skillet over medium heat for 8–10 minutes, breaking into small chunks with back of spoon while cooking. Cook until evenly browned and completely cooked.
2. Drain to reduce fat.
3. Add to pasta sauce, chili, casseroles, tacos or soup, seasoning to taste.
4. When adding frozen cooked ground beef to recipes calling for browned ground beef, you may need to slightly increase the recipe's cooking time.

Consider cooking up convenience when you stock up on ground beef. By cooking the meat before freezing, you will have cooked ground beef ready to add to your favourite pasta sauce, chili, soup, or casserole recipe. After cooking and draining the ground beef, freeze it on foil-lined baking trays, then scoop meal-sized portions into freezer containers. Freeze portions for up to 3 months. Dinner just got easier!

Ground Beef Safety Smarts

✓ Cook or freeze ground beef the day you buy it. Raw or cooked ground beef can be frozen for up to 3 months.
✓ Never thaw ground beef at room temperature. Thaw in the fridge, allowing 12–15 hours per pound (26–33 hours per kg). Cook microwave-thawed ground beef immediately. Thawed ground beef must be cooked before refreezing.
✓ Never eat ground beef rare. Cook ground beef thoroughly to 160°F (71). Ground beef can look done (no longer pink inside) before being completely cooked. Use a digital rapid-read thermometer to know your burger is safe and cooked to perfection. Just remember: Your burger's done at 71!

What's New at the Marketplace?

Ground Beef: Cooked frozen ground beef is ground beef that has been cooked, drained and then frozen. It's easy to add to your favourite pasta sauce, casseroles and soups, and it makes for super-simple shortcut meals. Also look for fully cooked frozen beef burgers.

Some plastic tray packages allow for longer storage times and are labelled with a "best before" date as a guide to storage time. Once opened, use or freeze the meat within one day. Tube or chub packaging is used for fresh or frozen ground beef. Use or freeze fresh meat chubs within a day. If there is a "best before" date on the package, use that as your guideline, but once opened, freeze or use the meat within one day.

Roasts: Bottom sirloin tri-trip is a flavourful, economical beef cut that has long been popular with Canadian restaurants and American consumers. This boneless cut comes as grilling steaks or medallions, or as triangular oven roasts, ranging from 1½ to 2 pounds (750 g–1 kg). Best cooked just to medium, trip-tip can be marinated 8–24 hours before cooking, for improved tenderness.

Quick roasts and premium quick roasts are boneless mini-beef roasts that suit hectic schedules and smaller family-sized appetites. With their even shape and small size (1 pound/500g), they can oven-roast in less than an hour.

Rotisserie roasts and premium rotisserie roasts are beef roasts for the barbecue. These boneless roasts are cut and tied in an even shape to promote uniform cooking and easy rotation on the rotisserie. They range in size from 4–13 pounds (2-6 kg) and can be cooked on a rotisserie spit or directly on the grill using an indirect cooking method.

Steaks: Grilling and marinating medallions are thicker-cut steaks that cook to perfection more easily than traditional steaks. This greater thickness makes it easier to achieve a range of doneness from rare to well done, and there's less chance of overcooking. As well, each medallion is portion-sized, so there's no need to cut a larger steak down to size to fit on the plate.

The Nutritional Benefits of Beef

Every satisfying mouthful of lean beef gives you energy and essential nutrients to help sustain you and your family even on your most active days. Lean beef gives you Z-I-P: *zinc* to boost your immune system and to promote children's healthy growth; *iron* to help carry oxygen throughout your body to fuel all your daily activities; *protein* to build and repair muscle and other tissue for a strong, healthy body; plus B vitamins to help release food energy and assist with many body functions.

Healthy Helpings: Canada's Food Guide to Healthy Eating recommends 2 to 3 servings (50–110 grams each) of meat and alternatives each day. However, nutrition surveys have found that many Canadians, especially women, eat less than the minimum of 2 servings from this food group. Eating fewer than the recommended servings may put you at risk for developing deficiencies of key nutrients such as iron, zinc and B vitamins. Enjoying 2–3 servings of meat and alternatives, such as lean beef, is an important part of healthy eating.

Heart Health: Lean beef can easily be part of heart-healthy eating, even if you're watching your blood cholesterol level. In fact, research shows that lean beef can be as effective as chicken or fish as part of a lower-fat diet to reduce blood cholesterol levels (according to the 1999 *Archives of Internal Medicine*).

Heart Healthy Tips

✓ Use added fats, such as oils, dressings, mayonnaise, gravy and cream sauces, in moderation.
✓ Choose leaner meats, such as lean, trimmed cuts of beef and lean or extra-lean ground beef. One serving of cooked meat (100 g) is about the size of a deck of cards.

✓ Cook the low-fat way. Broil, barbecue, roast or microwave on a rack, or steam or stir-fry in a non-stick pan.

✓ Eat plenty of high-fibre foods, such as whole-grain breads and cereals, beans, peas and lentils.

✓ Include colourful vegetables and fruit as sources of antioxidant nutrients plus fibre.

✓ Enjoy regular physical activity to keep your heart fit and to maintain a healthy weight.

✓ Avoid smoking and excessive alcohol intake.

Did you know that about two-thirds of the fat in beef is either unsaturated or in the form of stearic acid, a saturated fatty acid shown to have little effect on blood cholesterol levels?

If you're concerned about fat, it's good to know that today's trimmed lean beef qualifies for the Heart and Stroke Foundation of Canada's Health Check program, designed to help Canadians make healthy food choices. All trimmed beef cuts, except short ribs, qualify for Health Check. In order to qualify, raw cuts must have no more than 10 percent fat. In fact, most cuts of beef qualify as extra-lean, with less than 7.5 percent fat when trimmed of visible fat.

Extra-Lean Raw Beef Cuts With Less Than 7.5 Percent Fat When Trimmed

Grilling Steaks: rib eye, rib, strip loin, T-Bone, Porterhouse, top sirloin, wing.
Marinating Steaks: eye of round, flank, inside round, outside round.
Oven Roasts: eye of round, inside round, outside round, rump, sirloin tip.
Premium Oven Roast: tenderloin.
Pot Roasts: blade, brisket, cross rib.
Simmering Steaks: blade.
Stewing Beef: stewing cubes.

Beef and Barley Soup

This delicious soup is worth the wait, but when in a rush, see the quick tip.

Servings: 4–6
Preparation: 30 minutes
Cooking: 2 hours

1 lb	500 g	simmering steak (beef cross rib or blade), stewing cubes or boneless simmering short ribs, cut in ¾-inch (2 cm) cubes
6 cups	1.5 L	vegetables, cut in small pieces (i.e., onions, carrots, celery, rutabaga and/or potatoes)
¼ cup	50 mL	pot or pearl barley
1	1	can (10 oz/284 mL) beef broth
¼ tsp	1 mL	each: dried thyme, dillweed and pepper
1	1	bay leaf

Trim beef cubes of external fat and brown in large non-stick pot. Add all other ingredients plus 4 cups (1 L) water and bring to a boil. Cover and reduce heat to simmer, cooking for about 2 hours until beef and barley are tender. Remove the bay leaf. Serve sprinkled with chopped fresh parsley, if desired.

TIP: To make this soup in a rush, mix 1 pouch (56 g) quick stew mix (usually sold at the meat case of most stores) with water according to package directions and marinate beef for 30 minutes. Meanwhile, bring all other ingredients listed above plus 3 cups (750 mL) water to a boil in a large pot. Cover, reduce heat and simmer for 15 minutes. Add beef and its marinade and cook covered for another 30 minutes until beef and barley are tender.

Nutrition Per Serving

357 Calories, 8.5 g Fat, 29 g Protein, 41 g Carbohydrates.
An excellent source of Iron (27% RDI) and Zinc (76% RDI)

Beef & Spinach Salad with Cream Cheese & Candied Pecans

For those occasions when you want to make an impression.

Servings: 4
Cooking: 20–25 minutes
Marinating: 12 hours

1 lb	500 g	inside or outside round marinating steak (or rib eye or strip loin grilling steak)
1 cup	250 mL	low-fat raspberry, huckleberry or balsamic vinaigrette dressing
¼ cup	50 mL	sugar
½ cup	125 mL	pecan pieces
		steak spice, to taste
1 bag	283 g	washed and trimmed fresh spinach
4 oz	125 g	Mascarpone, chèvre, Ricotta or other cream cheese

Marinate steak with ½ cup (125 mL) salad dressing in resealable freezer bag (12 hours for marinating steak/10–15 minutes for grilling steak). Discard marinade. Candy-coat pecans by heating with sugar for 2 minutes in heavy frypan over high heat, stirring constantly until sugar is melted and becomes golden and syrupy. Be careful not to burn pecans. Immediately remove pan from heat and use 2 forks to scoop the candied pecans onto a plate covered with waxed paper to cool. (This whole process takes only 3–4 minutes and requires caution.) Season steak with your favorite steak spice and broil, barbecue or pan-fry steak for 4–5 minutes per side, to desired doneness. Cut steak in thin slices across the grain. Just before serving, toss spinach with ½ cup (125 mL) salad dressing. Place on plates and top with slices of cooked steak, crumbled cream cheese and pecans. Sprinkle with freshly ground pepper, if desired.

Nutrition Per Serving
521 Calories, 36 g Fat, 26 g Protein, 25 g Carbohydrates.
An excellent source of Iron (29% RDI) and Zinc (62% RDI)

Beef Salad on the Wild Side

A hearty salad that's great served either warm or cold.

Servings: 6
Preparation: 10–15 minutes
Cooking: 45–60 minutes

1 cup	250 mL	uncooked wild rice or wild rice blend
4 tsp	20 mL	instant chicken soup mix
1½ cups	375 mL	bagged broccoli slaw (or mixture of small broccoli flowerets & carrot slices)
¼ cup	50 mL	walnut pieces (optional)
½	½	large red bell pepper, cut in strips
4	4	green onions, thinly sliced
¾ cup	175 mL	Jalapeno Jack, Havarti or Gouda cheese, cut into small cubes
3 cups	375 g	shaved or thinly sliced cooked roast beef, cut into strips
¾ cup	175 mL	fat-reduced honey dijon salad dressing
2 tbsp	30 mL	lemon juice
1–2 tsp	5–10 mL	curry powder
		Freshly ground pepper to taste

Rinse rice with hot water; drain. Meanwhile, in medium saucepan, bring 3 cups (750 mL) water to a boil. Add rice and soup mix; bring back to boil. Reduce heat to low, cover and simmer 45–60 minutes or until most of water is absorbed and rice is tender. Drain any remaining liquid and let cool slightly. In large bowl, toss next 6 ingredients with rice. In 1 cup (250 mL) measure, combine dressing, lemon juice and curry powder. Pour over rice mixture and toss gently. Sprinkle with pepper. Serve immediately while still warm or cover and refrigerate to chill before serving.

Nutrition Per Serving

398 Calories, 15 g Fat, 30 g Protein, 36 g Carbohydrates.
A good source of Iron (24% RDI) and an excellent
source of Zinc (61% RDI)

Chinese Steak Salad

A variety of enticing textures and flavours make this a terrific one-dish meal.

Servings: 4–6
Preparation: 10–15 minutes
Cooking: 10 minutes

½ cup	125 mL	pineapple juice
½ cup	125 mL	teriyaki marinade or sauce
2 tbsp	30 mL	sesame oil
1½ tsp	7 mL	grated fresh ginger root or ½ tsp (2 mL) ground ginger
4 cups	1 L	cooked roast beef or cooked top sirloin grilling steak (approximately 500 g), sliced in ¼-inch strips
1	1	bag (14 oz/454 g) coleslaw (bagged cabbage and carrot mixture)
1	1	package (250 g) frozen Chinese pea pods (rinsed and drained to defrost) or 1 cup (250 mL) fresh snow peas
2	2	packages (3 oz/85 g) instant Oriental soup noodles (beef flavour) broken up
⅓ cup	75 mL	shelled, salted sunflower seeds

Prepare dressing by combining powdered soup packet from 1 package of noodles with the first 4 ingredients. (Save other powdered soup packet for another recipe). Pour ½ cup (125 mL) dressing over sliced cooked steak in plastic zipper bag and marinate in the refrigerator for about 10 minutes. Meanwhile, bring remaining dressing to a boil. Toss vegetables, noodles and seeds with hot dressing. Top with steak and dressing mixture. Garnish with sliced red pepper, if desired. Serve with crusty rolls.

Nutrition Per Serving

389 Calories, 18 g Fat, 25 g Protein, 32 g Carbohydrates

Dijon Beef and Greens

Greens become gourmet in just 15 minutes when savory beef meets Dijon.

Servings: 4
Preparation: 10 minutes
Cooking: 10 minutes

1 lb	500 g	sirloin or strip loin steak
3 tbsp	45 mL	Dijon mustard
½ tsp	2 mL	cracked pepper
2 tbsp	30 mL	each: red wine vinegar and mayonnaise
½ tsp	2 mL	each: sugar and crushed garlic
1	1	package (300 g) mixed salad greens
		prepared croutons

Reserve 2 tbsp (30 mL) mustard. Spread remainder on steak and top with pepper. Broil or grill steaks, about 5 minutes per side for medium. Meanwhile whisk together reserved mustard, vinegar, mayonnaise, sugar and garlic. Toss greens with dressing, reserving 2 tbsp (30 mL) dressing for topping. Divide greens onto serving plates, top with croutons. Slice steaks into thin strips, place on greens and drizzle with reserved dressing.

Nutrition Per Serving

218 Calories, 9.1 g Fat, 28 g Protein, 5.1 g Carbohydrates

Ginger Beef Salad

Tasty and quick, this recipe is sure to become a family favourite.

Servings: 4
Preparation: 5–10 minutes
Cooking: 5 minutes

¼ cup	50 mL	apricot jam
1 tbsp	15 mL	grated fresh ginger root
1 tsp	5 mL	minced garlic
1 tbsp	15 mL	Hoisin or soy sauce
1 lb	500 g	beef stir-fry strips (or inside round or sirloin tip marinating steak, cut into strips)
½	½	pouch honey garlic or hot 'n spicy coating mix
8 cups	2 L	mixed baby greens or bagged salad greens

In small saucepan over low heat, melt jam and stir in ginger root, garlic and Hoisin sauce. Shake beef strips in bag containing coating mix. Stir-fry beef in preheated lightly-oiled skillet over medium-high heat for 2–3 minutes. Pour jam mixture over beef, stirring for 1–2 minutes to coat strips. Serve immediately over your favourite mixed greens.

Nutrition Per Serving

256 Calories, 7.1 g Fat, 27 g Protein, 20 g Carbohydrates

Italian Beef Soup

A quick solution for a busy weeknight meal.

Servings: 4–5
Preparation: 5 minutes
Cooking: 15 minutes

1 lb	500 g	beef stir-fry strips or fast-fry steak, cut into thin strips, 1½-inch (4cm) long
3 tbsp	45 mL	Worcestershire sauce
1	1	can (28 oz/796 mL) stewed tomatoes
1	1	can (12 oz/341 mL) canned corn
1 cup	250 mL	beef broth
1	1	large clove garlic, minced
1 tsp	5 mL	dried basil
¼ cup	50 mL	thinly sliced fresh basil (optional)
		grated Parmesan cheese (optional)

Toss beef with 2 tbsp (30 mL) Worcestershire sauce, set aside. In large saucepan combine tomatoes, corn (including liquid), broth, garlic, dried basil, remaining 1 tbsp (15 mL) Worcestershire sauce and pepper to taste. Bring to boil; cover and reduce heat to low. Simmer 5-10 minutes. Turn heat off and stir in beef; cover and let stand 5 minutes to cook beef. Stir in fresh basil and garnish with cheese, if desired. Serve immediately with crusty bread.

TIP: Substitute 1 tsp (5 mL) dried oregano for dried basil and fresh cilantro or parsley for fresh basil.

Nutrition Per Serving

253 Calories, 5.5 g Fat, 25 g Protein, 30 g Carbohydrates

Japanese Steak Salad

Full flavour and convenience for today's busy lifestyle.

Servings: 4–6
Preparation: 10–15 minutes
Marinating: 30 minutes–2 hours

1 cup	250 mL	bottled Japanese dressing
2 tbsp	30 mL	sesame oil
4 cups	1 L	cooked round marinating steak, blade simmering steak or top sirloin grilling steak (approx 1 lb/500 g) or cooked roast beef (or 500 g deli roast beef), sliced in ¼-inch/ 5mm strips
1	1	bag (14 oz/454 g) coleslaw (shredded cabbage and carrots)
1	1	package (250 g) frozen pea pods (rinsed and drained to defrost) or 1 cup/250 mL) fresh snow peas
2	2	packages (3 oz/85 g each) instant Oriental soup noodles, broken up (don't use powdered soup packets)
⅓ cup	75 mL	shelled, salted sunflower seeds

Combine Japanese dressing and sesame oil. Pour ½ cup (125 mL) dressing over sliced cooked beef in plastic zipper bag and marinate in the refrigerator for about 30 minutes to 2 hours before cooking. Meanwhile, bring remaining dressing to a boil. Toss vegetables, noodles and seeds with hot dressing. (Save powdered soup packets for another recipe). Top with steak and dressing mixture. Garnish with sliced red pepper, if desired. Serve with crusty rolls.

TIP: A marinating or simmering steak (such as round, sirloin tip, cross rib or blade) would work well in this recipe. Simply marinate beef in bottled Japanese dressing for two hours before cooking. To allow noodles to be a little less crunchy, chill for 15–30 minutes before serving. If using deli roast beef (which tends to be saltier), use unsalted sunflower seeds.

Nutrition Per Serving
413 Calories, 20 g Fat, 35 g Protein, 23 g Carbohydrates.
An excellent source of Iron (29% RDI) and Zinc (67% RDI)

Layered Mediterranean Loaf

Add this dish to your next buffet. Your guests will be glad you did!

Servings: 8
Preparation: 20 minutes
Cooking: 15–30 minutes (optional)

2 cups	500 mL	thick and chunky salsa
1 tbsp	15 mL	dried sweet basil
¼ cup	50 mL	canned, sliced pimientos (drained)
½ cup	125 mL	sliced, pitted ripe olives
1	1	10-inch (25cm) round Italian, sour dough or pumpernickel bread loaf
½ lb	250 g	cooked roast beef or deli roast beef (2 cups/500 mL), very thinly sliced
1 cup	250 mL	finely shredded mozzarella cheese

Combine the first 4 ingredients in a medium bowl. Cut the loaf in half horizontally. Leaving a 1-inch (2.5 cm) border, scoop out a ½-inch (1 cm) layer from the inside of each half. Spread the salsa mixture evenly over both halves, including border. On the bottom half, layer half the cheese, all of the beef, and top with remaining cheese. Pack filling down slightly. Carefully invert the top half onto the bottom half. Press down firmly on the loaf and wrap tightly in plastic wrap. Store the loaf in the refrigerator for 15–30 minutes (or overnight) between 2 plates with something heavy on top to keep the loaf flattened. Serve sliced in wedges with your favourite salad or, to serve warm, wrap in foil and place in preheated 300ºF (150ºC) oven for 15–30 minutes until cheese melts.

Nutrition Per Serving
219 Calories, 4 g Fat, 14 g Protein, 31 g Carbohydrates.
An excellent source of Iron (29% RDI) and a good source of Zinc (23% RDI)

Mediterranean Pasta Salad with BBQ Roast Beef

Wonderful flavours that team perfectly with barbecued or oven roasted beef.

Servings: 8
Preparation: 20 minutes
Cooking: 1–1½ hours

3 lb	1.5 kg	premium oven roast (top sirloin or rib eye)
2 cups	500 mL	fusilli or penne pasta
½ cup	125 mL	light mayonnaise
1	1	package or bottle sundried tomato Parmesan pasta sauce/seasoning
2 tbsp	30 mL	lemon juice
2	2	green onions, sliced
½ cup	125 mL	each: diced red pepper and thinly sliced zucchini
⅓ cup	75 mL	feta cheese, crumbled (optional)
¼ cup	50 mL	sliced black olives (optional)

Season roast to taste and insert meat thermometer into centre of roast. Preheat BBQ to medium-high heat. Grill, fat side up, or cook on rotisserie over drip pan in closed BBQ over indirect heat. Allow from 20 minutes/lb (45 minutes/kg) for rare to 30 minutes/lb (65 minutes/kg) for well done. Meanwhile, cook pasta according to package directions, rinse under cold running water, drain well. In large bowl, combine mayonnaise, seasoning mix and lemon juice. Stir in drained pasta, onions, red pepper and zucchini, toss to coat. Cover and chill at least 1 hour. Toss with feta cheese and sliced black olives, if desired. Serve as a side dish with the thinly sliced roast beef.

TIP: To oven roast, place roast, fat side up, on rack in roasting pan without lid. Season roast to taste and insert meat thermometer into centre of roast, avoiding fat or bone. Roast at 325°F (160°C) to desired doneness, allowing from 20 minutes/lb (45 minutes/kg) for rare to 30 minutes/lb (65 minutes/kg) for well done.

Nutrition Per Serving

325 Calories, 12 g Fat, 31 g Protein, 18 g Carbohydrates

Pomegranate & Citrus Beef Salad

Tasty, refreshing and exotic — sure to become a favourite main-course salad.

Servings: 4
Preparation: 15 minutes
Cooking: 12 minutes
Marinating: 30 minutes

1	1	pomegranate
3	3	dried figs
1	1	clove garlic
¼ cup	50 mL	white wine vinegar
		salt and pepper
1 lb	500 g	beef marinating steak (inside round, sirloin tip or flank), 1-inch (2.5 cm) thick
1	1	pink grapefruit
8 cups	2 L	mixed baby greens or bagged salad greens
1	1	jar (6 oz/170 mL) marinated artichokes, drained
½ cup	125 mL	thinly sliced red or green onion

Place half the seeds from pomegranate into blender, reserving remaining seeds. Add figs, garlic and vinegar to blender; blend until paste-like. Season with salt and pepper to taste; place in large sealable freezer bag. Pierce beef all over with fork. Add to freezer bag and refrigerate 30 minutes. Meanwhile, cut peel and pith off grapefruit. Separate and reserve sections, collecting and squeezing out juice from membranes; set sections aside and reserve juice. Discard marinade and grill or broil steak using medium-high heat, 6–7 minutes/side for medium. Slice beef thinly across the grain. Divide salad greens among 4 serving plates; top with beef strips, grapefruit sections, artichoke hearts and onion. Drizzle each with Citrus Dressing and garnish with reserved pomegranate seeds.

Citrus Dressing: Add enough white wine vinegar to reserved grapefruit juice to make ½ cup (125 mL). Whisk in 2 tbsp (30 mL) olive oil, 2 tbsp (30 mL) each liquid honey and chopped fresh mint and ½ tsp (2 mL) grainy Dijon mustard; season with salt and pepper to taste.

Nutrition Per Serving

315 Calories, 13 g Fat, 27 g Protein, 26 g Carbohydrates.
An excellent source of Iron (27% RDI) and Zinc (52% RDI)

Potstickers

These tasty morsels are a real crowd pleaser!

Servings: 5–10, or 40 potstickers
Preparation: 40–45 minutes
Cooking: 10 minutes

1 cup	250 mL	cooked roast beef (or 125 g deli roast beef), coarsely chopped
½ cup	125 mL	shredded green cabbage (or bagged coleslaw)
1	1	plum tomato, cut in chunks
¼ cup	50 mL	green onions, chopped
½ cup	125 mL	BBQ sauce (e.g., honey garlic flavour)
1 tbsp	15 mL	each: minced ginger and ginger
		hot sauce to taste
1 tsp	5 mL	each: cumin and cornstarch
1	1	400 g package of 3-inch (7.5 cm) wonton wrappers
1	1	whisked egg
2 tbsp	30 mL	toasted sesame seeds
1 cup	250 mL	each: BBQ sauce (e.g., honey garlic flavour) and light sour cream

Using food processor, combine first 8 ingredients for filling. Lay wonton wrappers on waxed paper and brush with whisked egg. Spoon approximately 1 tsp (5 mL) of filling onto center of each wrapper. Fold up wrapper and pinched closed like a perogy. In large pot, boil first 20 potstickers for about 3 minutes and remove with a slotted spoon. Repeat with remaining potstickers. Gently transfer cooked potstickers to large pan containing mixture of BBQ sauce and light sour cream. Heat for 3 minutes. For a spicier sauce, add 1 tbsp (15 mL) bottled hot garlic, ginger and chili. Serve potstickers and sauce sprinkled with sesame seeds, allowing 3–4 per person as an appetizer (or 6–8 for a meal).

Tip: For a spicier sauce, add 1 tbsp (15 mL) bottled hot garlic, ginger and chili.

Nutrition Per Serving
170 Calories, 3.9 g Fat, 8.9 g Protein, 24 g Carbohydrates.
A source of Iron (14% RDI) and a source of Zinc (11% RDI)

Spicy Beef & Rice Salad

This hot Waldorf-like salad, with its variety of textures and flavours, will add some zip.

Servings: 4
Cooking: 25–30 minutes

1½ tsp	7 mL	chili powder
½ tsp	2 mL	ground cumin
¼ tsp	1 mL	garlic powder
⅛ tsp	.5 mL	dried oregano leaves
		dash cayenne pepper
1 lb	500 g	grilling steak (such as top sirloin, rib eye, tenderloin), cut 1-inch (2.5 cm) thick
1 cup	250 mL	bagged or boxed wild rice blend
2–3	2–3	green onions, thinly sliced
1	1	red apple, cut into pieces
2	2	stalks of celery, finely sliced
½ cup	125 mL	apple juice
¼ cup	50 mL	coarsely chopped walnuts, toasted, if desired

Mix first 5 ingredients to prepare spice seasoning. Rub 1 tsp (5 mL) of the mixture into both sides of the steak. Prepare rice according to package directions with water, salt and butter. Stir in remaining spice seasoning from above. Bring to a boil, cover and simmer for 20 minutes. Combine green onions, cut apples, celery and apple juice and set aside. While rice is cooking, heat a large, non-stick skillet over medium heat for 5 minutes. Place steak in the skillet and cook 12–14 minutes for rare to medium, turning once (6–7 minutes per side). Remove to a plate. When rice is done, fold in onion/apple juice mixture and toss well. Carve steak into thin slices and arrange over the rice salad. Sprinkle top with toasted walnut pieces. Garnish with leaf lettuce and additional apple slices, if desired.

Nutrition Per Serving

340 Calories, 9 g Fat, 29 g Protein, 36 g Carbohydrates

Spinach Salad with Steak and Strawberries

An excellent way to host a do-ahead barbecue for those weeknight get-togethers.

Servings: 4
Marinating: 3 hours
Preparation: 20 minutes

1 lb	500 g	marinating steak (inside round, eye of round or flank)
2 tbsp	30 mL	white wine vinegar
1 tbsp	15 mL	Worcestershire sauce
1 tbsp	15 mL	finely chopped onion
1 tbsp	15 mL	sesame seeds
1 tsp	5 mL	sugar
1	1	clove garlic
½ tsp	2 mL	chili powder
¼ tsp	1 mL	white pepper
1 tbsp	15 mL	vegetable oil
1	1	bunch fresh spinach leaves, cleaned and stemmed
2	2	medium oranges, peeled
2 cups	500 mL	sliced fresh strawberries

Barbecue steak over medium hot coals, 5–6 minutes per side for rare, or until desired doneness. Slice across grain into thin slices; place on glass dish. To prepare marinade, combine vinegar, Worcestershire sauce, onion, sesame seeds, sugar, garlic, chili powder and pepper. Beat well with wire whisk or use blender. Gradually add oil, blending until smooth. Pour over steak slices, cover and refrigerate 3 hours or more. Place spinach on serving plate. Arrange beef slices, oranges and strawberries on spinach. Drizzle with remaining marinade.

Nutrition Per Serving
281 Calories, 9 g Fat, 30 g Protein, 23 g Carbohydrates

Tangy Thai Beef Pinwheels

These attractive appetizers are great for when you're entertaining.

Servings: 8–12
Preparation: 20–30 minutes

½ lb	250 g	cooked steak or roast beef, chilled and cut thinly *
1 cup	250 mL	bottled Thai sauce
1	1	small carrot, finely shredded
2	2	sweet red bell peppers, finely diced
2	2	green onions, finely diced
¼ cup	50 mL	fresh basil, finely chopped
2 tbsp	30 mL	fresh cilantro, finely chopped
8	8	white or colored tortillas (8 inches/20 cm in diameter)

Place cooked beef in a resealable bag and marinate with ¼ cup (50 mL) of Thai sauce for 10 minutes. Combine chopped vegetables, basil and cilantro with another ¼ cup (50 mL) of Thai sauce. Add beef mixture and mix well. Top tortillas with vegetable-beef mixture. Tightly roll up filling, folding in sides after first roll to enclose mixture. Continue until all mixture is used. Cut in 1-inch (2.5 cm) slices to serve as pinwheel appetizers (secure with toothpicks, if necessary) or cut in halves to serve as "wraps." Serve with bottled Thai sauce for dipping.

Variation: Tortillas may be spread with cream cheese before spreading with vegetable-beef mixture. These may be made up to 24 hours in advance.

* Recommend deli roast beef (cut in thin strips) — you need very thin slices to keep pinwheels from breaking.

Tip: Appetizers could be made up to 24 hours in advance to allow rolls to firm up and hold shape.

Nutrition Per Serving
181 Calories, 3.4 g Fat, 8.4 g Protein, 29 g Carbohydrates

Teriyaki Surf & Turf Salad

A fast and tasty meal mixed and served in a refrigerator container.

Servings: 4
Preparation: 10 minutes
Cooking: 15 minutes

1	1	can (14 oz/398 mL) pineapple chunks
¼ cup	50 mL	bottled teriyaki sauce
¾ cup	175 mL	instant rice (or 1 cup/250 mL leftover rice)
1 cup	250 mL	frozen peas
¼ cup	50 mL	each: chopped green onion and fresh cilantro
½ cup	125 mL	chopped celery
1	1	can (106 g) salad shrimp, drained
2 cups	500 mL	cooked beef (or 250 g deli roast beef), sliced
½	½	pkg (6 oz/170 g) chow mein noodles

Drain pineapple, reserving juice. Combine pineapple juice with teriyaki sauce. Cut roast beef into strips, combine with ¼ cup (50 mL) teriyaki/pineapple mixture in large freezer bag and chill in refrigerator. Prepare instant rice according to package instructions, omitting salt. While rice is hot, place in large (4 cup/946 mL) refrigerator container and mix with remaining ingredients, except beef and chow mein noodles. Marinate at least 10 minutes in refrigerator or overnight. Arrange rice mixture on plates, top with chow mein noodles and marinated beef strips.

Tip: For a picnic in the park, transport rice mixture in a large refrigerator container and beef strips in a freezer bag, with an ice pack in between.

Nutrition Per Serving

457 Calories, 13 g Fat, 34 g Protein, 52 g Carbohydrates

Thai Beef Wraps

These wraps can also be sliced to make about 40 pinwheel appetizers.

Servings: 4
Preparation: 20–30 minutes

1 cup	250 mL	Thai or other Asian flavoured sauce
½ lb	250 g	cooked steak or roast beef (e.g., deli roast beef), chilled and cut into thin slices
1	1	small carrot, finely shredded
2	2	each: sweet red peppers and green onions, finely diced
¼ cup	50 mL	fresh basil, finely chopped
2 tbsp	30 mL	fresh cilantro, finely chopped
8	8	plain or flavoured tortillas (8 inches/20 cm in diameter)

Place cooked beef in resealable bag and marinate with ¼ cup (50 mL) of the Asian sauce for 10 minutes. In small bowl, combine chopped vegetables, basil and cilantro with ¼ cup (50 mL) of the Asian sauce. Add beef mixture; mix well. Divide vegetable-beef mixture evenly among tortillas. For each wrap, fold in both ends and then lightly roll up tortilla. Cut each wrap in half (secure with toothpicks, if necessary) and serve immediately with remaining sauce for dipping.

Tip: Tortillas may be spread with cream cheese before spreading with vegetable-beef mixture. As well, these wraps can be tightly wrapped and refrigerated for up to 24 hours.

Nutrition Per Serving

549 Calories, 10 g Fat, 26 g Protein, 87 g Carbohydrates

Vietnamese Soup

This fragrant, delicious and healthy soup makes a quick meal in a bowl.

Servings: 4
Preparation: 15 minutes
Cooking: 40 minutes

8 cups	2 L	beef stock
2	2	shallots, minced
1 tbsp	15 mL	peeled, grated ginger root (½-inch/1 cm slice)
1 tsp	5 mL	ground Chinese 5 spice mixture
2	2	whole cloves
1 lb	500 g	grilling steak (top sirloin or tenderloin), frozen for 30 minutes for easier slicing
8 oz	250 g	rice stick noodles, vermicelli or ¼-inch (5 mm) wide flat noodles
2 tbsp	30 mL	oyster sauce
¼ tsp	1 mL	pepper
1½ cups	375 mL	fresh bean sprouts
2	2	green onions, thinly sliced
		lime wedges, fresh torn basil or cilantro leaves and sliced red or green chilies as condiments

In large saucepan over high heat, combine stock, shallots, ginger, Chinese 5 spices and cloves; bring to boil. Reduce heat to medium; simmer covered for 30 minutes. Remove and discard cloves. Meanwhile, use cleaver or large knife to slice beef across the grain on diagonal into paper-thin slices 2 inches (5 cm) long. (If slicing ahead of time, place slices on a plate; cover tightly and refrigerate). Soak noodles in hot water for 15 minutes; drain. Add oyster sauce, pepper and drained noodles to stock and bring to boil for 3 minutes or until noodles are tender. Divide beef slices, bean sprouts and green onions equally among 4 large soup bowls. Carefully ladle some of the boiling hot stock into each bowl to cook the beef. Serve with lime wedges, basil, cilantro and red or green chilies as condiments, if desired.

Nutrition Per Serving

422 Calories, 6 g Fat, 34 g Protein, 56 g Carbohydrates

Warm Beef & Berry Salad

This delicious main course salad celebrates the summer's berry crop.

Servings: 8
Preparation: 20 minutes
Cooking: 1–1½ hours
Marinating: 12–24 hours

⅔ cup	150 mL	each: olive oil and white wine vinegar
½ cup	125 mL	each: raspberry jam and apricot jam
2 tbsp	30 mL	liquid honey
1 tsp	5 mL	Dijon mustard
2	2	garlic cloves, minced
		Salt and pepper to taste
2 lb	1 kg	beef oven or rotisserie roast (e.g., inside round, outside round or sirloin tip)
1	1	large mango, peeled and sliced
2 cups	500 mL	summer berries (raspberries, blueberries or quartered strawberries)
12 cups	3 L	mixed salad greens

Combine oil, vinegar, raspberry jam, apricot jam, honey, mustard, garlic, salt and pepper. Place half the mixture in large sealable freezer bag, reserving the rest as dressing. Pierce roast all over with fork, add to bag and refrigerate 12–24 hours. Place drip pan containing ½-inch (1 cm) water under grill on one side of barbecue. Preheat barbecue to medium-high heat (400°F/200°C). Discard marinade and insert meat thermometer into centre of roast. Place roast on grill over drip pan; turn heat off under just the roast. Cook at constant heat, in closed barbecue, until thermometer reads 135°F–145°F (57°C–63°C) for rare to medium rare (about 1–1½ hours). Remove roast to cutting board; tent with foil 10–15 minutes. Carve roast into thin slices and toss with mango, berries, salad greens and reserved dressing.

TIP: The roast can be cooked with a rotisserie if you have one.

Nutrition Per Serving
342 Calories, 14 g Fat, 25 g Protein, 31 g Carbohydrates.
A good source of Iron (22% RDI) and an excellent
source of Zinc (48% RDI)

All Kinds O' Meatballs

The grated carrot keeps these lean meatballs juicy and gets kids eating vegetables.

Servings: 4–6
Preparation: 20 minutes
Cooking: 15 minutes

1 lb	500 g	lean ground beef
1	1	egg, lightly beaten
½ cup	125 mL	dry bread crumbs
⅓ cup	75 mL	each: finely grated carrot and shredded onion
1 tbsp	15 mL	Worcestershire sauce
½ tsp	2 mL	each: salt and pepper

Lightly combine all ingredients; form into about 30 1-inch (2.5 cm) balls. Bake on lightly oiled foil-lined baking tray in 400°F (200°C) oven for 15 minutes, until digital rapid-read thermometer inserted into centre of several meatballs reads 160°F (71°C).

Variations. Try adding the following to the basic recipe:

Italian: 2 tbsp (30 mL) pizza sauce and 1 tsp (5 mL) dried oregano. Serve with extra pizza sauce or spaghetti sauce.

Asian: 2 tbsp (30 mL) hoisin sauce and ½ tsp (2 mL) ground ginger. Serve with peanut sauce or sweet and sour sauce.

Mexican: 1 tbsp (15 mL) chili powder and 2 garlic cloves (minced). Serve with salsa.

Nutrition Per Serving
170 Calories, 10 g Fat, 14 g Protein, 6 g Carbohydrates

Beef Moussaka

The authentic flavour of a traditional Greek dish in a simplified version.

Servings: 6
Preparation: 25–30 minutes
Cooking: 45 minutes

1	1	large onion, chopped
1 lb	500 g	lean ground beef
1 tbsp	15 mL	tomato paste
2 tbsp	30 mL	fresh parsley, chopped
½ cup	125 mL	beef stock
4 tbsp	60 mL	breadcrumbs
2	2	eggplants (approx. 6–8 inches/ 15–20 cm each)
⅓ cup	75 mL	Parmesan cheese, grated
1	1	package (25 g) Bechamel or white sauce mix
1 cup	250 mL	milk

Cook onions with ground beef, stirring until browned. Add tomato paste, parsley and beef stock, salt and pepper to taste, and simmer for 15 minutes, uncovered. Stir in 3 tbsp (45 mL) breadcrumbs. Set aside. Meanwhile, prepare sauce by combining sauce mix with milk and cooking until thickened. Grease a 9-inch (22 cm) square casserole. Cut eggplants in ⅜-inch (1 cm) slices. To assemble moussaka, place a layer of eggplant slices on the bottom, add half of the ground beef mixture and sprinkle with half Parmesan cheese. Repeat and end with a layer of eggplant. Pour sauce over top and sprinkle with remaining Parmesan and breadcrumbs. Bake in 350°F (180°C) oven for 45 minutes.

Nutrition Per Serving

296 Calories, 15 g Fat, 21 g Protein, 20 g Carbohydrates

Beef Tart-ieres

Tasty meat pies that can be made ahead and frozen for reheating later.

Makes: 24 appetizers
Preparation: 15–20 minutes
Cooking: 30 minutes

24	24	frozen ready-to-bake mini tart shells (2 inches/5 cm)
1 lb	500 g	lean ground beef
½ cup	125 mL	instant rice
1	1	egg
1	1	pouch spicy onion soup/recipe mix
1 tbsp	15 mL	crunchy (or smooth) peanut butter
½ cup	125 mL	fruity steak sauce, Chinese sweet & sour sauce or seafood cocktail sauce

Separate tart shells and place on large baking sheet. Combine ground beef with rice, egg, onion soup mix and peanut butter. Press about 1 tbsp (15 mL) of meat mixture into each tart shell. Top each tart with about 1 tsp (5 mL) sauce and bake in preheated 375°F (190°C) oven for 30 minutes. Let stand 5 minutes before serving.

Nutrition Per Serving

113 Calories, 6.5 g Fat, 4.9 g Protein, 8.6 g Carbohydrates

Curried Beef and Lentils

This zinc-rich curry dish is best made with dried cooked lentils.

Servings: 5–6
Preparation: 20 minutes
Cooking: 10 minutes

4 tsp	20 mL	mild, medium or hot curry powder
¼ tsp	1 mL	each: dried chili pepper and ground cumin
1 tbsp	15 mL	vegetable oil
1	1	each: onion and celery stalk, diced
1 cup	250 mL	each: small cauliflower florets and grated carrot
1	1	garlic clove, minced
1 tbsp	15 mL	red wine vinegar
1 lb	500 g	lean ground beef
½ tsp	2 mL	dried thyme
1	1	plum tomato, diced
1½ cups	375 mL	cooked green lentils
3 tbsp	45 mL	fresh lemon juice
		Salt and freshly ground pepper
		Chopped fresh corinader

In a large deep skillet, toast curry powder, chili pepper and cumin using medium-high heat for 30 seconds or until fragrant. Add oil, onion, celery, cauliflower, carrot and garlic; cook, stirring for 3 minutes until vegetables begin to brown. Add vinegar, ground beef and thyme to pan, stirring up any browned bits from the bottom of the pan. Break up beef into small chunks with back of wooden spoon; cook 5–6 minutes until browned. Stir in tomato and lentils; heat through. Just before serving, stir in the lemon juice and season with salt and pepper to taste. Garnish with coriander and serve with hot cooked rice.

TIP: To prepare lentils, cook ⅔ cup (150 mL) dried geen lentils at a simmer in 1½ cups (375 mL) salted water for about 30 minutes or until just soft but not mushy.

Nutrition Per Serving
263 Calories, 13 g Fat, 20 g Protein, 17 g Carbohydrates.
An excellent source of Iron (28% RDI) and Zinc (47% RDI)

Empañadas de Picadillo

Serve as a tapas course or make larger-sized versions for a main course.

Servings: 8
Preparation: 15 minutes
Cooking: 10–15 minutes

2	2	garlic cloves, minced
1	1	onion, minced
½	½	sweet pepper, finely diced
1 lb	500 g	lean or extra lean ground beef
1 cup	250 mL	salsa
1 tbsp	15 mL	chili powder
1 tsp	5 mL	ground cumin
¾ cup	175 mL	sliced green olives (chopped if making tapas-sized empañadas)
½ cup	125 mL	raisins
		Salt and pepper
4	4	frozen pie shells, thawed
1	1	egg, lightly beaten

Cook garlic, onion, diced pepper and ground beef in a large skillet using medium heat, stirring occasionally for 8–10 minutes until beef is browned and completely cooked. Drain if necessary. Add salsa, chili powder and cumin; reduce heat to medium-low and simmer 3–4 minutes. Remove from heat; stir in olives and raisins. Season to taste and cool completely. Cut each pie shell in half to make main course empañadas. Form each of the 8 pastry pieces into a ball; roll out each into a 7-inch (18 cm) round. Use ½ cup (125 mL) ground beef mixture for each empañada. Moisten pastry edges with water; fold over and seal with fork. Place empañadas on parchment paper or foil-lined baking sheet; prick and brush each with beaten egg. Bake in 425°F (220°C) oven for 10–15 minutes or until golden brown.

Nutrition Per Serving

557 Calories, 34 g Fat, 16 g Protein, 48 g Carbohydrates

Greek Beef Bruschetta

A new twist on a popular appetizer. Perfect for casual entertaining.

Makes: 48 appetizers or 16 pizza wedges
Preparation: 10 minutes
Marinating: 5 minutes

1 lb	500 g	lean ground beef
1 tsp	5 mL	each: lemon pepper, basil and garlic powder
1	1	package (10 oz/300 g) frozen chopped spinach, thawed and squeezed dry
1	1	can (14 oz/398 mL) Italian seasoned diced tomatoes
½ cup	125 mL	grated mozzarella cheese
2	2	12-inch/30 cm flatbreads or pre-baked pizza crusts
1¼ cup	300 mL	seasoned crumbled feta cheese (200 g package)
½ cup	125 mL	sliced pitted ripe olives

Scramble-fry the beef and seasonings in a non-stick skillet until the beef is browned. Stir in the chopped spinach, canned tomatoes and mozzarella cheese. Remove from the heat. Lay pizza flatbreads on ungreased pizza pans. Spread beef mixture over flatbreads. Sprinkle with feta cheese and olives. Place under a preheated broiler 4–6 inches (10–15 cm) from the heat. Broil for 5 minutes or until hot and starting to brown on the edges. Let stand for a few minutes before cutting into small wedges or triangles for appetizers.

Nutrition Per Serving

78 Calories, 2.7 g Fat, 4.5 g Protein, 8.9 g Carbohydrates

Hearty Beef Pizza

Pizza is always the perfect choice for the family, and for the kids' lunchboxes.

Servings: 6
Preparation: 15 minutes
Cooking: 12–15 minutes (optional)

¾ lb	375 g	lean ground beef
1	1	large onion, chopped
1 tbsp	15 mL	Worcestershire sauce
1 tbsp	15 mL	dried basil
1 cup	250 mL	sliced mushrooms
1	1	can (7½ oz/213 mL) pizza sauce
1	1	pre-baked pizza crust (12–14 inches/30–35 cm)
1 cup	250 mL	chopped red and green peppers
2 cups	500 mL	grated mozzarella cheese or pizza cheese mixture

In skillet, brown ground beef with onion, about 5 minutes. Drain fat, if any. Stir in Worcestershire sauce, basil and mushrooms; cook for another 2–3 minutes. Spread pizza sauce evenly over crust. Layer half the cheese over sauce, then top with beef mixture, peppers and remaining cheese. Place pizza directly on rack in preheated 425°F (220°C) oven and bake for 12–15 minutes or until cheese is melted.

TIP: For a spicier flavour, add 1–2 tsp (5–10 mL) hot pepper flakes to beef mixture or use spicy pizza sauce.

Nutrition Per Serving

365 Calories, 17 g Fat, 23 g Protein, 30 g Carbohydrates

International Burgers

Chart a new course in burger flavours with these unusually tasty combinations.

Servings: 4–6
Preparation: 5 minutes
Cooking: 10 minutes

1 lb	500 g	medium ground beef
1	1	egg, beaten
¼ cup	50 mL	dry bread crumbs or small flake oatmeal

Combine ground beef with beaten egg, bread crumbs or oatmeal and one of the seasoning mixes below. Shape into 4–6, ¾-inch (2 cm) thick, evenly shaped, flat patties. Don't over mix. Broil or grill until well-done (centres are no longer pink) about 5 minutes/side, turning only once.

Mexi-Grill Burger: Mix in ⅓ cup (75 mL) salsa, 1 tsp (5 mL) chili powder and ½ (2 mL) tsp dried mustard. Top with onions, cheddar or Monterey Jack cheese and corn relish. Serve in a flour tortilla or onion bun.

Greek Burger: Mix in 1 tsp (5 mL) each garlic powder and rosemary and 1 tbsp (15 mL) oregano. Top with crumbled feta cheese, chopped black olives, tomatoes, onions, cucumbers and tzatziki sauce. Serve in a pita pocket.

Middle East Burger: Replace breadcrumbs with instant rice and mix in with ¼ cup (50 mL) chopped onion, 2 tbsp (30 mL) each raisins and slivered almonds and 1 tsp (5mL) curry powder. Top with mild chutney sauce. Serve with Naan bread or in a sesame bun.

TIP: Using medium ground beef rather than lean is more economical and makes juicier burgers. Low-fat cooking methods, such as broiling or barbecuing allow fat to drip away.

Nutrition Per Serving

207 Calories, 12 g Fat, 19 g Protein, 3.5 g Carbohydrates

Korean Beef with Lettuce Cups

This Asian-inspired recipe lets you entertain with style and within budget.

Servings: 6
Preparation: 10 minutes
Cooking: 15 minutes

3	3	garlic cloves, minced
½	½	sweet red pepper, diced
1 lb	500 g	lean ground beef
1 tsp	5 mL	minced ginger root
¼ cup	50 mL	soy sauce
1 tbsp	15 mL	Asian chili sauce
1 tsp	5 mL	sesame oil
1	1	head Bibb lettuce, separated into individual leaves
		Wedges fresh lime, Hoisin sauce, chopped green onion, shredded carrot or cucumber and chopped cilantro or mint

Cook garlic, diced pepper, ground beef and ginger root in large skillet using medium heat, stirring occasionally for 8–10 minutes, until browned and completely cooked. Drain if necessary. Add soy sauce, chili sauce and sesame oil; reduce heat to medium-low and simmer 3–4 minutes.

Transfer to warm platter. At the table, let each person spoon the filling into lettuce leaves, top with a squeeze of lime juice, and add some favourite toppings. Simply pick up and eat by hand.

TIP: If you want a more traditional dish, serve the Korean Beef mixture over steamed rice with a drizzling of hoisin sauce to complete. As an appetizer course, spoon warm beef mixture into endive lettuce leaves.

Nutrition Per Serving

179 Calories, 11 g Fat, 16 g Protein, 3 g Carbohydrates

Layered Cuban Dip

For a delightfully different appetizer, try this colourful layered party dip.

Makes: 12–15 appetizers
Preparation: 15 minutes
Cooking: 10 minutes

1 lb	500 g	extra lean ground beef
1 tsp	5 mL	cumin
1 tsp	5 mL	dried oregano
1	1	jar (320 mL) thick and chunky salsa (medium or hot)
¼ cup	50 mL	raisins (plumped in hot water)
1 cup	250 mL	light spreadable cream cheese, softened
½ cup	125 mL	fat-free sour cream
1	1	can (14 oz/398 mL) crushed pineapple, well drained
¼ cup	50 mL	each: finely chopped green onions and pimiento or red pepper

Brown ground beef with seasonings for 5 minutes on high in large skillet. Drain off fat and blot well with paper towel. (This is important to final appearance of recipe). Add salsa and raisins and cook 5 minutes on low. Meanwhile, combine cream cheese and sour cream and spread over a serving plate that has an edge. Top with hot beef mixture, well-drained pineapple, chopped green onions and pimiento. Serve immediately (or chill and serve) with rice crackers or sliced pita/flatbread.

Nutrition Per Serving

119 Calories, 4.1 g Fat, 8 g Protein, 7 g Carbohydrates

Make-Ahead Mexican Lasagna

Some like it hot with spicy salsa and jalapeños stirred into the tomato sauce.

Servings: 6
Preparation: 15 minutes
Cooking: 35 minutes

1	1	each: garlic clove and onion, chopped
1 lb	500 g	lean ground beef or ground chuck
1 tbsp	15 mL	chili powder
1 tsp	5 mL	ground cumin
1	1	9 oz/540 mL can kidney beans, drained and rinsed
1 cup	250 mL	light or regular sour cream
2 tbsp	30 mL	all-purpose flour
1	1	7½ oz/213 mL can tomato sauce
½ cup	125 mL	salsa
3	3	large flour or corn tortillas
1 cup	250 mL	shredded Cheddar cheese
½ cup	125 mL	each: sliced green olives and crushed tortilla chips
¼ cup	50 mL	sliced pickled jalapeño peppers, chopped (optional)

Cook garlic, onion, ground beef, chili powder and cumin in large skillet using medium heat, for 10 minutes until beef is browned and completely cooked. Drain if necessary. Stir in beans; set aside. Combine sour cream and flour until smooth; set aside. Combine tomato sauce and salsa; set aside. Place one and a half tortillas in the bottom of lightly oiled 2 qt (2 L) rectangular baking dish, overlapping slightly. Top with half each, meat mixture, sour cream mixture and tomato sauce mixture. Repeat layers. Bake in 350°F (180°C) oven for 30 minutes until bubbly. Top with cheese, olives, chips and jalapeño (if using) and bake 5 minutes longer.

TIP: To make ahead, cover uncooked lasagna tightly and refrigerate for up to 24 hours. Or over-wrap with foil and freeze for up to 2 weeks. Thaw in refrigerator for 48 hours before baking at 350°F (180°C) for about 50 minutes. Add toppings and finish baking.

Nutrition Per Serving

550 Calories, 26 g Fat, 33 g Protein, 47 g Carbohydrates

Meatballs with Roasted Vegetables and Garlic

This easy oven meal dresses up meatballs for any occasion.

Servings: 5
Preparation: 20 minutes
Cooking: 1 hour

12 cups	3L	mixed vegetable pieces (i.e., thick potato and onion wedges, thick carrot or parsnip slices, turnip sticks)
8	8	large cloves garlic, halved
1 tbsp	15 mL	olive oil
1½ tsp	7 mL	dried rosemary
1	1	red pepper, cut into thick wedges
		Cooked meatballs*

In large non-stick roasting pan toss mixed vegetables and garlic with oil, rosemary, 1 tsp (5 mL) salt, ½ tsp (2 mL) pepper; spread out into single layer. Roast in 375°F (190°C) oven for 35–40 minutes or until almost tender. Stir in red pepper and meatballs; continue roasting about 20 minutes or until vegetables are tender.

* Mix 1 lb (500 g) extra lean ground beef with 1 egg, ½ cup each dry bread crumbs and finely chopped onion, ½ tsp each salt and pepper and 1 tbsp Worcestershire sauce; shape into 1-inch (2.5 cm) balls. Arrange in single layer in shallow baking pan; bake in 500°F (260°C) oven for 8–10 minutes or until no longer pink in center.

TIP: To speed up preparation purchase ready-to-serve meatballs or prepare as directed ahead of time; cook, cool and refrigerate or freeze individually on trays and then seal in air tight bags for up to 3 months. Leave the skin on the potatoes for more fibre and colour.

Nutrition Per Serving

389 Calories, 11 g Fat, 27 g Protein, 46 g Carbohydrates

Japanese Steak Salad   page 25

Mediterranean Pasta Salad with BBQ Roast Beef page 27

The Prairie Burger   page 52

All Kinds O' Meatballs page 37

Korean Beef with Lettuce Cups   page 45

Mexican Hot Pot   page 49

Thai Beef Wraps page 34

Moroccan Spiced Quick Roast with Kasbah Couscous   page 77

Mexican Hot Pot

This satisfying one-pot meal takes only 17 minutes from start to finish.

Servings: 4
Preparation: 5 minutes
Cooking: 12 minutes

1 lb	500 g	lean ground beef
1	1	package (35 g) taco seasoning mix
1¾ cups	425 mL	extra mild or mild thick 'n chunky salsa
1 cup	250 mL	beef broth
½ cup	125 mL	instant rice
2 cups	500 mL	frozen mixed vegetables

Brown beef in a large saucepan; drain any remaining fat. Add seasoning mix, salsa, broth, and 4 cups (1L) of water. Bring to a boil. Stir in rice, cover and cook about 5 minutes. Stir in vegetables and heat through. Serve with nachos.

TIP: Substitute soup pasta for rice and simmer just until pasta is tender.

Nutrition Per Serving

427 Calories, 13 g Fat, 29 g Protein, 49 g Carbohydrates

M-M-Marvellous Mushroom Burgers

The mushrooms in this recipe keep these lean ground beef burgers moist and juicy.

Servings: 4
Preparation: 20 minutes
Cooking: 12 minutes

1 lb	500 g	extra lean or lean ground beef
1	1	egg, beaten
¼ cup	50 mL	each: dried bread crumbs and finely chopped mushrooms
1	1	medium onion, finely diced
3	3	garlic cloves, minced
1 tsp	5 mL	each: dried oregano and basil
¼ tsp	1 mL	each: salt and pepper

Combine ground beef, egg, bread crumbs, mushrooms, onion, garlic, oregano, basil, salt and pepper. Mix lightly and shape into 4–6 patties, ¾-inch (2 cm) thick. Grill, broil or pan-fry using medium-high heat for 5–7 min/side, until digital rapid-read thermometer inserted sideways into centre of each patty reads at least 160°F (71°C). At this temperature, patties are cooked regardless of colour. Serve burger patties on toasted whole-wheat buns with low-fat toppings like shredded lettuce, sliced tomatoes, dill pickle slices, mustard and ketchup.

Nutrition Per Serving
254 Calories, 14 g Fat, 24 g Protein, 7 g Carbohydrates.
A good source of Iron (19% RDI) and an
excellent source of Zinc (56% RDI)

Muffin-Sized Pizza Meat Loaves

These little meat loaves are the perfect size and flavour for children's meals.

Servings: 6
Preparation: 15 minutes
Cooking: 30 minutes

1½ lb	750 g	lean ground beef
1	1	egg, beaten
½ cup	125 mL	finely shredded carrot (1 large)
⅓ cup	75 mL	finely shredded onion (1 small)
¼ cup	50 mL	fine dry bread crumbs
1 tsp	5 mL	dried oregano
½ tsp	2 mL	salt
¼ tsp	1 mL	pepper
½ cup	125 mL	pizza sauce

Vegetable Sauce

1 tbsp	15 mL	olive oil
1 cup	250 mL	each: diced sweet red pepper and zucchini
⅔ cup	150 mL	pizza sauce

In large bowl, combine beef, egg, carrot, onion, bread crumbs, oregano, salt, pepper and ¼ cup (50 mL) of the pizza sauce. Mix lightly but thoroughly to blend. Divide mixture among 12 muffin cups, pressing into cups. Divide remaining pizza sauce among meat loaves, spooning some sauce on top of each. Bake in 375°F (190°C) oven for 25–30 minutes or until instant-read thermometer inserted into centre of a meat loaf registers 160°F (71°C). Serve with Vegetable Sauce.

Vegetable Sauce: In skillet, heat oil over medium-high heat; add red pepper and zucchini, cook stirring occasionally until softened. Add pizza sauce and heat through.

Nutrition Per Serving

297 Calories, 17 g Fat, 24 g Protein, 12 g Carbohydrates

The Prairie Burger

Loaded with prairie ingredients, this moist and delicious burger is a very popular

Servings: 4
Preparation: 20 minutes
Cooking: 12–16 minutes

1 lb	500 g	medium ground beef
½ cup	125 mL	quick cooking rolled oats
¼ cup	50 mL	each: light sour cream and finely minced brown or white button mushrooms
1	1	medium onion, finely diced
3	3	garlic cloves, minced
1 tbsp	15 mL	each: Dijon mustard and chopped fresh parsley (or 1 tsp/5 mL dried)
1 tsp	5 mL	each: dried oregano and thyme
¼ tsp	1 mL	salt and fresh cracked pepper

In large bowl, combine beef, rolled oats, sour cream, mushrooms, onion, garlic, parsley, mustard, oregano, thyme, salt and pepper. Mix lightly but thoroughly to blend. Shape into 4 to 6, ½- to ¾-inch thick (1–2 cm) patties. Lightly oil grill. Barbecue, broil or pan-fry using medium-high heat for 5–7 minutes per side (turning once) until instant-read thermometer inserted sideways into centre of patties reads at least 160°F (71°C). Patties cooked to an internal temperature of 160°F (71°C) are completely cooked, regardless of colour. Serve on toasted whole wheat buns, topped with Speedy Cabbage Slaw as a relish.

Speedy Cabbage Slaw: In large bowl, whisk together ⅓ cup (75 mL) each: white wine vinegar and sugar, ¼ cup (50 mL) canola oil, 1 tbsp (15 mL) each: Dijon mustard and chopped fresh parsley. Add 16 oz/454 g bagged coleslaw mix (or 4 cups/1 L) shredded cabbage and carrots) and 1 finely sliced red onion; toss well. Cover and let stand for two hours at room temperature or up to one week in refrigerator.

Nutrition Per Serving

504 Calories, 22 g Fat, 29 g Protein, 49 g Carbohydrates

Simple Meat Sauce

Tag this recipe and keep it in the kitchen for your everyday family meals.

Servings: 4
Preparation: 15 minutes
Cooking: 40 minutes

1 tbsp	15 mL	olive oil
1	1	onion, diced
1	1	garlic clove, minced
1 cup	250 mL	diced vegetables (e.g., zucchini and sweet pepper)
1 lb	500 g	ground beef
1	1	can (28 oz/796 mL) tomatoes
1	1	can (5½ oz/156 mL) tomato paste
1 tbsp	15 mL	brown sugar
½ tsp	2 mL	dried oregano
		salt and pepper

Heat oil in large, heavy saucepan using medium heat. Add onion, garlic, vegetables and ground beef; cook, stirring occasionally, for 8–10 minutes, until beef is browned and completely cooked. Drain. Add tomatoes, tomato paste, sugar and oregano. Break up tomatoes with back of spoon. Bring to a boil, stirring often, reduce heat to low; cover and simmer for 30 minutes, stirring occasionally. Season with salt and pepper to taste, and add a bit more sugar if necessary. Serve over hot pasta.

TIP: You can make a rich beef ragù. When adding tomatoes to the meat sauce, stir in ½ cup (125 mL) each pitted black olives (chopped) and dry red wine, and ½ tsp (2 mL) dried chili pepper flakes. Serve topped with freshly grated Parmesan cheese.

Nutrition Per Serving
305 Calories, 18 g Fat, 19 g Protein, 20 g Carbohydrates.
An excellent source of Iron (26% RDI) and Zinc (43% RDI)

Spiced Beef Stuffed Peppers

Raisins give this delicious spiced beef filling a hint of sweetness.

Servings: 4
Preparation: 15 minutes
Cooking: 50–55 minutes

4	4	medium sweet peppers (mixed colours)
1 lb	500 g	extra lean ground beef
½ cup	125 mL	each: chopped onion and carrot
2	2	cloves garlic, minced
½ cup	125 mL	cooked rice
¼ cup	50 mL	raisins
2 tsp	10 mL	chili powder
¼ tsp	1 mL	each: cinnamon and hot pepper flakes
1	1	can (14 oz/398 mL) tomato sauce

Cut tops from peppers; discard seeds and membranes. Chop enough of the tops to make ½ cup (125 mL). In lightly oiled non-stick skillet, cook beef, chopped peppers, onion, carrot and garlic, until beef is no longer pink. Remove from heat and drain fat, if any. Stir in rice, raisins, seasonings, ½ tsp (2 mL) salt and ½ cup (125 mL) tomato sauce. Spoon evenly into peppers. Place upright in shallow baking dish, large enough to hold peppers in single layer and pour remaining sauce around peppers. Cover tightly and bake at 350°F (180°C) for 45–50 minutes or until peppers are tender-crisp.

Nutrition Per Serving

343 Calories, 12 g Fat, 26 g Protein, 34 g Carbohydrates

Greek Steak Sandwich

This hearty refreshing sandwich is best eaten with a knife and fork.

Servings: 4
Preparation: 5 minutes
Cooking: 4 minutes

1 lb	500 g	beef fast-fry minute steak, cut in four pieces
1 tsp	5 mL	each: garlic powder and black pepper
½ cup	125 mL	low fat yogurt
¼ cup	50 mL	light mayonnaise
½ cup	125 mL	each: diced cucumber and tomato
2 tsp	10 mL	dried oregano
¼ tsp	1 mL	salt
4–8	4–8	Boston or butter lettuce leaves
2	2	greek-style pita bread (no pocket pita), halved
		Crumbled feta cheese and sliced black olives (optional)

Sprinkle both sides of steak with garlic powder and pepper. Mix yogurt, mayonnaise, cucumber, tomato, oregano and salt together; set aside. In large non-stick or lightly oiled skillet, brown steaks about 1–2 minutes each side. Cover pita with lettuce, top each with steak and spoon sauce over steak. Sprinkle cheese and olives on top, if desired.

Variation: Add ¼ tsp (1 mL) dried dillweed and ¼ cup (50 mL) sliced green onion.

TIP: For a different version, toss torn greens with sauce and thin slices of cooked steak and wrap in pitas or tortillas or serve as a salad.

Nutrition Per Serving

321 Calories, 12 g Fat, 30 g Protein, 22 g Carbohydrates

Harvest Beef Kabobs

It takes only five common ingredients to create this truly five star flavour!

Servings: 4
Preparation: 20 minutes
Cooking: 10 minutes

1½ cups	375 mL	honey mustard or honey garlic BBQ sauce
2 tsp	10 mL	chili powder
1 lb	500 g	beef grilling kabobs or top sirloin grilling steak, cut into one-inch cubes
1	1	medium pepper squash (1½ lb/750 g)
2	2	red peppers

In medium bowl mix BBQ sauce and chili powder. Set aside about ½ of sauce. Add beef cubes to remaining sauce in bowl, turning to coat. While cubes are marinating, pierce squash several times and microwave on high for 4–5 minutes until just partially cooked. Cool slightly. Halve, seed and cut peppers and squash into 1½ inch (4 cm) pieces. Alternately thread beef cubes and vegetables onto metal skewers or soaked wooded skewers. Brush vegetables with reserved sauce and place kabobs on greased grill or under broiler. Close lid and cook for about 10–12 minutes until squash is crisp-tender and meat is medium rare. Turn kabobs occasionally and brush generously with reserved marinade throughout cooking.

Nutrition Per Serving

299 Calories, 6.8 g Fat, 24 g Protein, 38 g Carbohydrates

Hawaiian Beef Stir-Fry

The classic stir-fry would not be complete without beef.

Servings: 4
Preparation: 15 minutes
Cooking: 10 minutes

½ tsp	2 mL	cornstarch
2 tbsp	30 mL	Worcestershire sauce, divided
1 lb	500 g	top sirloin grilling steak, cut into ¾-inch (2 cm) cubes
¼ cup	50 mL	ketchup
1 tbsp	15 mL	sugar
1	1	can (398 mL) pineapple chunks
1	1	green or red sweet pepper, cut into ¾-inch (2 cm) pieces
1–2	1–2	cloves garlic, minced, or ½ tsp (2 mL) garlic powder

In medium bowl, dissolve cornstarch and 1 tbsp (15 mL) Worcestershire sauce. Add beef cubes and toss to coat. In small bowl mix ketchup, sugar and 1 tbsp (15 mL) each Worcestershire sauce and juice from pineapple for sauce; drain pineapple. Brown beef in a large oiled skillet over medium-high heat. Remove and set aside. In same skillet heat 2 tbsp (30 mL) water over medium-high heat; add peppers and garlic. Cook and stir 3–4 minutes or until water evaporates and peppers are crisp-tender. Reduce heat and stir in sauce mixture, pineapple and beef along with any accumulated juices. Heat through and serve over hot rice.

Nutrition Per Serving

254 Calories, 4.7 g Fat, 22 g Protein, 32 g Carbohydrates

Mediterranean Beef Stir-Fry

These popular flavours are bound to be a hit with family and friends alike.

Servings: 4
Cooking: 30 minutes

1 lb	500 g	beef stir-fry strips
1	1	large onion, sliced thinly
½	½	jar (375 mL) pimento stuffed green olives, drained and coarsely chopped
1	1	jar (170 mL) marinated artichoke hearts
1 cup	250 mL	sundried tomatoes, snipped in pieces

Pour boiling water over sundried tomatoes, cover and set aside. Skim 2 tsp (10 mL) marinating oil from jar of artichokes and place in non-stick pan with onion. Cover and sauté for 10 minutes or until browned. Remove onions from pan and stir-fry beef strips until no longer pink. Meanwhile drain artichoke hearts, reserving ¼ cup (50 mL) marinade. Drain sundried tomatoes and add them to beef in pan along with artichoke hearts, reserved marinade, olives and onions. Simmer uncovered for 10 minutes, stirring occasionally, allowing flavours to blend and liquid to reduce. Serve with broad egg noodles, orzo or risotto and colourful mixed vegetables.

Nutrition Per Serving

339 Calories, 19 g Fat, 28 g Protein, 16 g Carbohydrates

Pizza-Style Minute Steaks

The popular flavours of beef and pizza combine for an easy meal the entire family

Servings: 4
Preparation: 5 minutes
Cooking: 15 minutes

1 lb	500 g	beef fast-fry minute steaks, cut in four pieces
1	1	each: medium green pepper and onion, chopped
1–2	1–2	cloves garlic, minced
1	1	can (14 oz/398 mL) pizza sauce or 1¾ cups (425 mL) of your favourite pasta sauce
1 cup	250 mL	shredded Italian cheese mixture (i.e., mozzarella, Parmesan)

Brown steaks in a large oiled skillet over medium-high heat about 1–2 minutes per side. Remove from skillet and set aside. Reduce heat to medium and add 2 tbsp (30 mL) water, green pepper, onion and garlic to skillet; cook and stir 2–3 minutes. Stir in pizza sauce and simmer 3–5 minutes to blend flavours. Return steaks and any accumulated juices to skillet and spoon sauce over top. Sprinkle cheese on top of steaks. Cover and heat 2–3 minutes or until cheese melts. Serve with pasta and salad or spread slices of toasted Italian bread with sauce and top with steaks for an open-faced sandwich.

TIP: For variety, try different vegetables, sauces and cheeses.

Nutrition Per Serving

299 Calories, 6.8 g Fat, 24 g Protein, 38 g Carbohydrates

Quick 'n Easy Beef Bourguignon

This updated version of the traditional favourite is slimmed down and simplified.

Servings: 4
Preparation: 15 minutes
Cooking: 10 minutes

1 lb	500 g	top sirloin grilling steak, thinly sliced
1	1	package (34 g) roasted garlic and red wine sauce mix
½ lb	250 g	whole small mushrooms or halved large
1	1	medium zucchini, thinly sliced
2 cups	500 mL	frozen baby carrots
¼ tsp	2 mL	pepper

In lightly oiled skillet, stir-fry steak over high heat for 3–4 minutes or until no longer pink. Meanwhile, whisk sauce mix and 1 cup + 2 tbsp (280 mL) water together; add sauce and vegetables to skillet. Bring to boil stirring constantly; reduce heat, cover and cook 5–7 minutes or until vegetables are just tender. Add salt to taste and serve over mashed potatoes or egg noodles.

Nutrition Per Serving

228 Calories, 5.3 g Fat, 25 g Protein, 21 g Carbohydrates

Sesame Ginger Beef Stir-Fry

A flavourful beef stir-fry is quick and easy with pre-cut vegetables.

Servings: 4
Preparation: 10 minutes
Cooking: 6–10 minutes

1 lb	500 g	beef stir-fry strips or top sirloin grilling steak, cut into strips
1 cup	250 mL	bottled light sesame ginger sauce
1	1	small cooking onion, sliced
1	1	pkg (500 g) international or Chinese-style frozen mixed vegetables (or 4 cups/1 L sliced assorted fresh vegetables)
½	½	large red or green bell pepper, cut in thin strips
¼ lb	125 g	oyster, shitake or crimini mushrooms, sliced

Heat a lightly oiled non-stick pan or wok over medium-high heat. Add 2 tbsp (30 mL) of sesame ginger sauce to beef strips before adding to pan, and stir-fry for 2–3 minutes. Remove beef from pan and set aside. Bring pan back to medium-high temperature. Add onion and stir-fry until softened. Add other vegetables and stir-fry for 2–3 minutes. Reduce heat and cover for 1 minute. Add remaining sauce and coat vegetables well. Return beef to pan and stir-fry until beef and vegetables are hot. Serve immediately with rice or fine noodles.

TIP: If desired, add green onions, water chestnuts and/or baby corn.

Nutrition Per Serving

328 Calories, 8.7 g Fat, 31 g Protein, 31 g Carbohydrates

Steak and Pepper Heroes

Similiar to a decadent cream cheese steak, but much lower in calories and fat.

Servings: 4
Preparation: 5 minutes
Cooking: 4 minutes

1 lb	500 g	beef stir-fry strips
1	1	large clove garlic, minced, or ½ tsp (2 mL) garlic powder
1	1	green or red pepper, cut into strips
1	1	onion, sliced
½ cup	125 mL	processed light cheese spread
1 tsp	5 mL	Worcestershire sauce
4	4	crusty Italian rolls, cut in half

Split rolls along one side; wrap in foil and warm in oven. Heat a large, lightly oiled skillet over medium heat, stir-fry beef and garlic for 2 minutes; remove beef. Add peppers and onion; stir-fry 2–3 minutes or until softened. Return beef and stir in cheese and Worcestershire sauce just to melt. Spoon mixture with sauce into rolls.

TIP: For a spicier version, substitute Mexican-flavoured cheese spread and omit Worcestershire sauce.

Nutrition Per Serving

385 Calories, 9.7 g Fat, 37 g Protein, 35 g Carbohydrates

Thai Beef Satay

This simple version of a traditional Thai favourite is great for appetizers.

Servings: 4
Preparation: 25 minutes
Cooking: 6–8 minutes

3 tbsp	45 mL	peanut butter
2 tbsp	30 mL	each: soy sauce and lemon juice
1 tbsp	15 mL	brown sugar
½ tsp	2 mL	each: minced garlic and ground ginger
¼ tsp	1 mL	crushed red chili pepper
1 lb	500 g	fast-fry minute steak or rouladen-cut marinating steak, cut into long strips ½ inch (1 cm) wide, or beef grilling kabobs

Soak wooden skewers in water for at least 10 minutes to prevent charring. In medium bowl, whisk together peanut butter, soy sauce, lemon juice, brown sugar, garlic, ginger and chili pepper. Whisk in 2 tbsp (30 mL) water until smooth. Stir in beef strips until coated. Let stand at room temperature for up to 15 minutes. Thread strips loosely onto wooden skewers. Broil or grill 3–4 minutes each side.

Nutrition Per Serving

244 Calories, 11 g Fat, 30 g Protein, 6.1 g Carbohydrates

Thai Spicy Beef with Noodles

The exotic flavour of Thailand made fast and easy.

Servings: 4
Cooking: 15 minutes

1 lb	500 g	beef stir-fry strips or top sirloin grilling steak, cut into strips
1	1	pkg (500 g) international Japanese style frozen vegetable mixture
1	1	pkg (1 oz/28.4 g) Thai spicy beef seasoning mix
2 cups	500 mL	broccoli slaw
1	1	small red pepper, cut into strips
1	1	pkg (400 g) Shanghai or Udon noodles

Preheat lightly oiled non-stick pan to medium-high heat and stir-fry beef strips until no longer pink. Remove beef strips from pan, add frozen vegetables and stir-fry 30 seconds. Reduce heat, cover vegetables and cook for 2–3 minutes. Meanwhile, prepare Thai spicy beef seasoning sauce as per package instructions. Turn heat up to medium-high and add remaining vegetables plus sauce, stir-fry for 2 minutes until sauce thickens. Add noodles and beef strips and continue to stir-fry until heated through.

TIP: For simple satays, prepare 1 package of seasoning mix as per package instructions and place in resealable freezer bag with 1 lb (500 g) beef strips. Marinate in refrigerator for 15 minutes. Weave strips accordion-style onto 8–10 bamboo skewers which have been soaked in water, using 3–4 beef strips per skewer. Broil or grill for 1–2 minutes per side, do not overcook. Skewers may be cut in 3–4 pieces to create appetizer satays or serve as a main dish over rice or Shanghai noodles.

Nutrition Per Serving

355 Calories, 6.6 g Fat, 31 g Protein, 41 g Carbohydrates

Asian Rotisserie Roast with Tropical Salsa

Asian flavours provide a touch of the exotic that's perfect for entertaining.

Servings: 16
Preparation: 10 minutes
Cooking: 2 hours (minimum)
Marinating: 2 hours (minimum)

½ cup	125 mL	each: soy sauce and rice vinegar
¼ cup	50 mL	liquid honey
1 tbsp	15 mL	Asian chili sauce
2 tsp	10 mL	each: sesame oil and finely shredded ginger root
4 lb	2 kg	beef rotisserie roast (cross-rib, inside round, outside round, sirloin tip) or premium rotisserie roast
		serve with Tropical Salsa (see below)

In large resealable freezer bag or bowl, combine soy sauce, vinegar, honey, chili sauce, sesame oil and ginger root. Pierce roast numerous times with long fork and add to bag; seal tightly and refrigerate 12–24 hours for rotisserie roast, or 2–4 hours for premium rotisserie roast. Discard marinade. Place drip pan under grill; add ½ inch (1 cm) water to pan. Preheat barbecue to medium-high (400°F/200°C). Cooking with rotisserie: insert spit rod lengthwise through centre of roast; secure with holding forks. Cooking without rotisserie: place roast on grill over drip pan moved to one side. Turn off the burner under roast. Insert meat thermometer into middle of roast avoiding spit rod (if using). With constant heat and closed barbecue, cook over drip pan until thermometer reads 155°F (68°C) for medium (about 30 min per lb/500 g). Remove to cutting board; tent with foil for 10 to 15 minutes to allow temperature to rise 5°F (3°C). Cut into thin slices across the grain.

Tropical Salsa: In blender, purée 1 peeled, pitted mango. Stir in ½ cup (125 mL) crushed pineapple, 1 tbsp (15 mL) each chopped fresh mint or coriander, granulated sugar, rice vinegar and 1½ tsp (7 mL) Asian chili sauce. Season with salt and pepper to taste.

Nutrition Per Serving
167 Calories, 6 g Fat, 22 g Protein, 6 g Carbohydrates.
A source of Iron (11% RDI) and an excellent
source of Zinc (39% RDI)

BBQ "Five Spiced" Beef Roast

Serve this roast with steamed Asian vegetables, rice and a sui choy salad.

Servings: 4–6
Preparation: 10 minutes
Cooking: 1 hour
Marinating: 12 hours

2 lb	1 kg	oven roast (sirloin tip, inside or outside round)
1 cup	250 mL	soy sauce
¼ cup	50 mL	liquid honey
2 tbsp	30 mL	each: minced ginger root and garlic
1 tbsp	15 mL	ground Chinese 5 spice
1 tbsp	15 mL	Sambal Oelek hot pepper condiment (or crushed chiles, to taste)

Pierce roast numerous times with fork. In plastic resealable freezer bag, combine remaining ingredients. Add roast to mixture in bag; seal tightly and refrigerate for 12 hours. Remove roast from bag; reserve marinade. Insert meat thermometer into middle of roast. Place roast in barbecue preheated to high; turn to low setting; close lid and cook to desired doneness. Meanwhile, boil reserved marinade for 5–10 minutes and use to baste roast at end of cooking time. For medium rare, roast will take approximately 1 hour to reach 145°F (62°C) internally. Remove roast to cutting board; tent with foil for 15 minutes before carving thinly across the grain.

TIP: To feed a crowd, use a 4–6 lb (2–3 kg) sirloin tip, inside or outside round rotisserie roast and double the amount of marinade ingredients. Barbecue roast over medium-high heat on rotisserie or by the indirect method for approximately 2–3 hours, using a meat thermometer to check doneness.

Nutrition Per Serving
237 Calories, 9.4 g Fat, 33 g Protein, 3 g Carbohydrates
A good source of Iron (21% RDI) and an
excellent source of Zinc (91% RDI)

Best BBQ Beef Oven Roast

Salad dressing makes a super easy marinade and offers lots of flavour options.

Servings: 11–12 (for 4lb/2kg roast)
Preparation: 10 minutes
Cooking: 1¼ hours
Marinating: 12–24 hours

4–13 lb	2–6 kg	beef rotisserie or oven roast (inside round, eye of round or sirloin tip)
2 cups	500 mL	salad dressing (e.g., balsamic vinaigrette or sun-dried tomato)

Pierce roast all over with fork. Place in large sealable freezer bag with dressing; refrigerate 12–24 h. Place drip pan, containing ½-inch (1 cm) water, under grill. Heat barbecue to 400°F (200°C), using medium-high heat. Discard marinade. Insert spit rod lengthwise through centre of roast; secure with holding forks. Insert meat thermometer into middle of roast, avoiding spit rod. Cook roast in closed barbecue over drip pan, maintaining constant heat, until thermometer reads 135°F-145°F (57°C-63°C) for rare to medium rare (about 18–21 min/lb or 40–47 min/kg). Remove roast to cutting board; tent with foil 10–15 min to allow temperature to rise 5°F (3°C). Carve into thin slices to serve.

Indirect Heat Barbecue Roasting: Cook roast directly on the grill positioned over a drip pan that is placed on one side of a preheated barbecue; turn heat off under just the roast. Cook in closed barbecue with constant heat (as above). Roast will cook slightly faster than on rotisserie.

TIP: In the summer months, enjoy beef roasts barbecued, using a rotisserie or the indirect heat method.

Nutrition Per Serving

200 Calories, 8 g Fat, 30 g Protein, .1 g Carbohydrates

Brandied Beef Tenderloin

This simple version of a French classic makes a very special dinner.

Servings: 6
Preparation: 5 minutes
Cooking: 40 minutes

1½ tsp	7 mL	cracked pepper
1 tbsp	15 mL	Dijon mustard
1½ lb	750 g	tenderloin premium oven roast (or prime rib, rib or striploin)
¼ cup	50 mL	milk
2 tbsp	30 mL	brandy
1	1	package (34 g) demi-glace gravy mix

Mix pepper and mustard; brush on all sides of roast. Place in small roasting pan or metal baking dish; roast in 325°F (160°C) oven until desired temperature is reached (140°F/60°C for rare or 160°F/71°C for medium) about 20–25 minutes per lb/500 g. Remove roast, tent with foil; add ¾ cup (175 mL) water, milk, brandy and sauce mix to roasting pan. Bring to boil, whisking constantly; reduce heat and simmer 1 minute. Serve sauce over thinly sliced tenderloin.

Nutrition Per Serving

180 Calories, 7.7 g Fat, 20 g Protein, 5.0 g Carbohydrates

Cajun Pot Roast

The rich flavour of this roast is enhanced by the colourful array of vegetables.

Servings: 12–15
Preparation: 30 minutes
Cooking: 3 hours

3-4 lb	1.5-2 kg	blade or cross rib pot roast
1 cup	250 mL	beef stock
1	1	can (14 oz/398 mL) Italian stewed tomatoes
¼ tsp	1 mL	cayenne
1	1	bay leaf
1 tbsp	15 mL	Worcestershire sauce
¾ cup	175 mL	each: chopped onions and celery
1	1	each: red and green pepper, chopped
6	6	carrots, cut into chunks
6	6	potatoes
1 cup	250 mL	each: frozen corn and okra (optional)

In large, lightly oiled pot, brown roast on all sides. Reduce heat and add remaining ingredients (except corn and okra). Simmer covered on stove or in 325°F (160°C) oven for 2½ hours. Season with salt to taste. Add corn and okra and cook covered for another 15 minutes. Remove roast and vegetables; discard bay leaf. Thicken juice left in pot with a paste made from 2 tbsp (30 mL) each of flour and water. Slice roast and serve with vegetables and sauce.

Nutrition Per Serving

222 Calories, 9.6 g Fat, 17 g Protein, 17 g Carbohydrates

Caribbean Quick Roast

The glazing sauce can also be served as a chutney to go with other roasts.

Servings: 2–3
Preparation: 5 minutes
Cooking: 55 minutes

½ cup	125 mL	canned crushed pineapple
2 tbsp	30 mL	steak sauce
½ tsp	2 mL	curry powder
¼ tsp	1 mL	ground ginger
⅛ tsp	0.5 mL	ground allspice or cloves
1	1	clove garlic, minced
½	½	green onion, finely chopped
½	½	small hot banana pepper, seeded and sliced (or ¼ tsp/1 mL cayenne pepper)
1	1	beef quick roast or premium quick roast (about 1 lb/500 g)

In small saucepan, combine pineapple, steak sauce, curry powder, ginger, allspice, garlic, onion and banana pepper. Simmer over medium heat, stirring occasionally for 5 minutes. Set aside ⅓ cup (75 mL) of this sauce mixture. Remove netting from roast. Insert meat thermometer lengthwise into centre of roast so that shaft is not visible. Place on rack in ovenproof skillet or shallow pan. Brush surface of roast with sauce mixture remaining in saucepan. Cook 1 lb (500 g) roast, uncovered, in 350°F (180°C) oven 50–60 minutes or until thermometer reads 155°F (68°C) for medium. Remove roast to cutting board; tent with foil for 5 minutes to allow temperature to rise 5°F (3°C). Cut into thin slices across the grain and serve with the reserved ⅓ cup (75 mL) sauce.

Nutrition Per Serving
246 Calories, 8 g Fat, 34 g Protein, 9 g Carbohydrates.
A good source of Iron (19% RDI) and an
excellent source of Zinc (52% RDI)

Festive Cranberry Pot Roast

The wonderful aroma of this roast matches its great taste.

Servings: 10–12
Preparation: 30 minutes
Cooking: 45–60 minutes

1	1	pouch quick stew mix
3 lbs	1.5 kg	pot roast (beef cross rib, blade or shoulder), trimmed of external fat
		Coarse black pepper to taste
10 cups	2.5 L	fresh, frozen or canned vegetables, cut in chunks (carrots, onions and potatoes)
3	3	whole cloves
½ (14 oz)	½ (398 mL)	can whole berry cranberry sauce
1	1	orange, juice and grated peel
½ tsp	2 mL	cinnamon

Pierce repeatedly through roast with a knife, long-tined fork or skewer. Place roast in large resealable freezer bag with quick stew mix, prepared according to package directions. Marinate for 30 minutes, turning over at half-time. Meanwhile, prepare vegetables and place in large pot. Add roast and marinade. Season with pepper and cloves. Bring to a boil, reduce heat and simmer covered, turning roast after 25 minutes. Cook until centre of roast registers at least 155°F (68°C) on a meat thermometer and meat is tender. Place roast and vegetables on a platter. Remove cloves and drain fat from drippings. Add last 3 ingredients to drippings and stir while heating. Thicken with a mixture of 2 tbsp (30 mL) each of cornstarch and cold water, if desired. Serve thin slices of roast, carved across the grain, with sauce and warm dinner rolls.

TIP: You can omit quick stew mix and brown roast on all sides in a large lightly oiled pot. Add 1 cup (250 mL) water and remaining ingredients (except vegetables) and cook covered for at least 3 hours on stovetop or in 325°F (160°C) oven. Add vegetables for the last half hour of cooking time.

Nutrition Per Serving

299 Calories, 9.5 g Fat, 26 g Protein, 27 g Carbohydrates

Herb & Mustard "Plastered" Rotisserie Roast

The sweetness of apples and the heat of jalapenos pair beautifully with grilled beef.

Servings: 6
Preparation: 20 minutes
Cooking: 1½–1¾ hours

2 lb	1 kg	premium rotisserie roast (prime rib or top sirloin) or oven roast (sirloin tip, eye of round or inside round)
¼ cup	50 mL	grainy or plain Dijon mustard
3	3	large cloves garlic, finely minced
1 tsp	5 mL	each: Worcestershire sauce and dried rosemary, oregano and thyme (or 1 tbsp/15 mL each fresh)
½ tsp	2 mL	freshly ground pepper
		serve with Apple Onion Salsa (see below)

Insert rotisserie rod lengthwise through centre of roast so that it is balanced; secure with holding forks. In small bowl, combine remaining ingredients to make a thick, spreadable paste. Set roast on spit rod over large bowl or pot; coat roast with mustard paste. Insert meat thermometer into centre of roast, avoiding spit rod. Place roast over drip pan in barbecue preheated to medium-high 400°F (200°C). Close lid; cook 45–55 minutes until thermometer reads 155°F (68°C) for medium. Remove to cutting board; tent with foil. Let stand 10–15 minutes; temperature will rise 5°F (3°C). Slice thinly across the grain.

Apple Onion Salsa: In medium bowl, combine 1 large McIntosh apple, cored and finely diced, 1 Roma tomato, seeded and diced, ⅓ cup (75 mL) chopped green onion, 2 tbsp (30 mL) each: apple cider vinegar and chopped cilantro or parsley, 1 tbsp (15 mL) horseradish, 3–4 tsp (15–20 mL, or to taste) finely minced fresh or pickled jalapeno peppers, 1 clove garlic, finely minced, and salt and pepper to taste. Mix well; let stand 30 minutes. Taste before serving; add herbs or seasonings, if needed. Makes about 1¾ cups (425 mL).

Nutrition Per Serving

215 Calories, 7.2 g Fat, 29 g Protein, 7.7 g Carbohydrates

Herb Medley Beef Roast

This flavourful roast is sure to please family and guests alike.

Servings: 10–12
Preparation: 10 minutes
Cooking: 1½–1¾ hours
Marinating: 12–24 hours

3 lbs	1.5 kg	oven roast (sirloin tip, eye of round, inside round or outside round)
1	1	bottle (344 mL) light herb medley marinade
		freshly ground black pepper
1 cup	250 mL	red wine (optional)
½ lb	250 g	mushrooms, sliced

Marinate roast in a large resealable freezer bag with ½ bottle of marinade for 12–24 hours. Remove roast from bag, season with pepper and place a meat thermometer into centre of roast. Discard used marinade. Preheat both sides of barbecue to medium heat. Place roast on grill, fat side up. Turn off flame under beef, or move beef away from direct heat. Close barbecue cover. During cooking period, baste roast twice with some of the remaining bottled marinade. Cook to an internal temperature of 140°F (60°C) for rare or 160°F (71°C) for medium. While roast is cooking, place wine and remaining marinade with mushrooms into a saucepan and cook over medium-high heat. Serve beef thinly sliced with sauce.

TIP: Can be prepared according to Oven Roast method.

Nutrition Per Serving

238 Calories, 9.5 g Fat, 27 g Protein, 10 g Carbohydrates

Holiday Roast with Portobello Sauce

Entertain in elegance with this sumptuous beef roast and mouth-watering sauce.

Servings: 8–12
Preparation: 20 minutes
Cooking: 2 hours

4 lb	2 kg	premium oven roast (prime rib or rib eye)
1	1	pouch (21 g) powdered cream of mushroom soup mix
2	2	portobello mushrooms
1 cup	250 mL	beef stock
2 tsp	10 mL	flour
1 tbsp	15 mL	balsamic or red wine vinegar

Place roast, fat side up, on rack in roasting pan without lid. Rub mushroom soup mix over surface of roast. Insert meat thermometer into centre of roast, avoiding fat or bone. Roast at 325°F (160°C) (see tip for roasting times). Remove roast from oven 5°F (2°C) below desired doneness temperature. Tent roast with foil and let stand for 10–15 minutes on cutting board before carving. Meanwhile, slice mushrooms ¼-inch (5 mm) thick; cut each slice in half lengthwise. Heat roasting pan over medium-high heat for 1 minute. Pour in beef stock, stirring to scrape up any brown bits. Add mushrooms and simmer 10 minutes. Mix flour with vinegar and whisk into pan. Bring to a boil, whisking constantly until thickened. Season with salt and pepper to taste. Serve roast and sauce with small roasted potatoes and steamed vegetables.

TIP: Rare — 20 min per lb/500g @ 140°F (60°C); *Medium* — 25 min per lb/500 g @ 160°F (71°C); *Well* — 30 min per lb/500 g @ 170°F (75°C).

Nutrition Per Serving

247 Calories, 16 g Fat, 22 g Protein, 2.9 g Carbohydrates

Italian Herb Roast

A succulent herb coating locks in the flavour and juiciness of this beef roast.

Servings: 10–12
Preparation: 10 minutes
Cooking: 1¾ hours

3 lbs	1.5 kg	oven roast (inside round, outside round, eye of round, sirloin tip or rump)
2 tbsp	30 mL	each: olive oil and minced garlic (6–8 cloves)
2 tsp	10 mL	each: basil, thyme and marjoram

Preheat oven to 500°F (260°C). Add water to roasting pan to a depth of ½ inch (1.2 cm). Place roast, fat side up, on a rack suspended over the water in the roasting pan. Mix oil, garlic and herbs and pat onto roast on all sides except bottom. Insert meat thermometer into centre of roast. Place uncovered roast in 500°F (260°C) oven for 30 minutes. Do not open oven door. Reduce heat to 275°F (140°C) and cook for about another 75 minutes for medium doneness (160°F/71°C internal temperature).

Nutrition Per Serving

208 Calories, 9.4 g Fat, 29 g Protein, 1 g Carbohydrates

Key Lime BBQ Beef Roast

Try this marinade for an incredibly flavourful and beautifully browned roast.

Servings: 8–10
Preparation: 5 minutes
Cooking: 1½ hours
Marinating: 12–48 hours

3 lbs	1.5 kg	oven roast (sirloin tip, inside round, eye of round, outside round or rump)
2 tbsp	30 mL	each: soy sauce and honey
½ tsp	2 mL	Tabasco sauce
¼ cup	50 mL	lime juice
1 tsp	5 mL	ground cumin
2 tbsp	30 mL	oyster sauce (optional)

Pierce roast numerous times with a fork. Combine marinade ingredients in shallow container or resealable freezer bag, reserving 2 tbsp (30 mL) of the marinade for basting roast while barbecuing. Marinate roast 12–48 hours in refrigerator. Discard used marinade. Insert meat thermometer into centre of roast. Grill fat side up or cook on rotisserie over drip pan in closed barbecue over indirect medium heat only to rare (i.e., internal temperature of 140°F/60°C) or medium (i.e., internal temperature of 160°F/71°C). Baste roast with the reserved marinade while barbecuing.

TIP: Premium Oven Roasts (i.e., sirloin, rib or tenderloin) can also be barbecued as above, but note that marinating is not required.

Nutrition Per Serving
196 Calories, 5.7 g Fat, 30 g Protein, 7.2 g Carbohydrates

Moroccan Spiced Quick Roast with Kasbah Couscous

This adventurous weeknight meal can be on the table with minimal time and effort.

Servings: 2–3
Preparation: 10 minutes
Cooking: 50 minutes

1 tsp	5 mL	each ground cinnamon, paprika, turmeric and garlic salt
½ tsp	2 mL	ground ginger
¼ tsp	1 mL	each: ground cumin, pepper and salt
1	1	beef quick or premium quick roast (approx 1 lb/500g) serve with Kasbah Couscous (see below)

In small bowl combine cinnamon, paprika, turmeric, garlic salt, ginger, cumin, pepper and salt. Remove netting from roast; rub some of the spice mixture evenly over roast. Insert meat thermometer lengthwise into centre of roast so that shaft is not visible. Place on rack in ovenproof skillet or shallow pan. Cook roast, uncovered, in 350°F (180°C) oven for 50–60 minutes, until thermometer reads 155°F (68°C) for medium. Remove roast to cutting board; tent with foil for 5 minutes to allow temperature to rise 5°F (3°C). Cut into thin slices across the grain and serve with hot Kasbah Couscous.

Kasbah Couscous: In medium saucepan, stir ½ cup (125 mL) couscous into ½ cup (125 mL) simmering chicken broth; remove from heat, cover and let stand 5 minutes. Gently stir in ¼ cup (50 mL) diced dried apricots or raisins, 1 green onion, chopped, 2 tbsp (30 mL) each Italian salad dressing and toasted slivered almonds and ½ tsp (2 mL) finely grated lemon peel. Season with salt and pepper to taste.

TIP: Any extra make-ahead rub can be stored in a sealed container for use on your next Moroccan Quick Roast or on your favourite beef Grilling Steak.

Nutrition Per Serving
150 Calories, 6 g Fat, 13 g Protein, 11 g Carbohydrates.
A good source of Iron (10% RDI) and
an excellent source of Zinc (23% RDI)

Pacific Rim Rotisserie Roast

This excellent marinade imparts a wonderful flavour while tenderizing.

Servings: 12–16
Preparation: 5 minutes
Cooking: 2–2½ hours
Marinating: 12–24 hours

4 lb	2 kg	rotisserie roast (inside round, outside round, eye of the round, sirloin tip or rump)
1 cup	250 mL	pineapple juice
½ cup	125 mL	each: soy sauce and packed brown sugar
¼ cup	50 mL	each: Worcestershire sauce, grated ginger root and honey mustard

Pierce roast numerous times with long fork. In large glass container or large re-sealable freezer bag, combine pineapple juice, soy sauce, brown sugar, Worcestershire sauce, ginger root and mustard. Add roast to container; cover and refrigerate, turning occasionally, for 8 to 24 hours. Discard marinade. Place drip pan under grill; add ½-inch (1 cm) water to pan. Using medium-high heat, preheat barbecue to 400°F/200°C. Insert spit rod lengthwise through centre of roast; secure with holding forks. Insert meat thermometer into middle of roast, avoiding spit rod. Maintaining constant heat, cook roast over drip pan in closed barbecue about 2 hours or until thermometer reads 155°F (68°C) for medium (about 30 minutes per lb/500 g). Remove roast to cutting board; tent with foil for 10–15 minutes to allow temperature to rise 5°F (3°C). Cut into thin slices across the grain.

TIP: *Indirect Heat Method*: Place roast on grill over drip pan on one side of barbeque. Turn heat off on side with roast. Cook as with rotisserie, turning roast every 30 minutes.

Nutrition Per Serving
137 Calories, 3 g Fat, 23 g Protein, 3 g Carbohydrates.
A good source of Iron (16% RDI) and
an excellent source of Zinc (43% RDI)

Roast Beef with Harvest Vegetables

Celebrate autumn with this delightfully different approach to an oven roast.

Servings: 6
Preparation: 15 minutes
Cooking: 1¼ hours

3 lb	1.5 kg	oven roast (eye of round, inside round, outside round or sirloin tip)
1 tsp	5 mL	each: powdered thyme, lemon juice, cracked pepper and seasoning salt
2 tsp	10 mL	balsamic vinegar

Vegetable Mix

1	1	each: red onion, red pepper and zucchini cut in thick slices
2	2	stalks celery, cut in 1-inch (2.5 cm) slices
1 cup	250 mL	frozen corn or corn cut from 2 fresh cobs
1 tbsp	15 mL	each: olive oil and lemon juice
1	1	sprig fresh rosemary
2 tbsp	30 mL	balsamic vinegar

Add water to roasting pan to a depth of ½-inch (1 cm). Place roast, fat side up, on a rack over water in pan. Mix topping ingredients together in a small bowl to make a paste. Spread on surface of roast and insert meat thermometer into centre of roast, avoiding fat or bone. Place uncovered roast in preheated 500°F (260°C) oven for ½ hour. Do not open oven door. Reduce heat to 275°F (140°C) and cook for another 1¼–1¾ hours for medium doneness (i.e., internal temperature of 160°F/70°C). Meanwhile, prepare vegetables and place in an oven-proof covered dish. Toss vegetables with olive oil, lemon juice and leaves from rosemary. Bake for 45 minutes along with roast at 275°F (140°C). Add vinegar to hot vegetables and serve over salad greens topped with roast beef slices. Serve with baby new potatoes.

Nutrition Per Serving

371 Calories, 13 g Fat, 46 g Protein, 16 g Carbohydrate

Rosemary Pot Roast with Braised Vegetables

This tender, slow cooked roast comes with its own side-dish of vegetables.

Servings: 10–12
Preparation: 10 minutes
Cooking: 3 hours

3 lb	1.5 kg	pot roast (cross rib, blade, shoulder or brisket)
		Salt and pepper
2	2	leeks or onions, coarsely chopped
10–15	10–15	baby potatoes (or 3–4 cups/750 mL–1 L peeled and cube potatoes)
1	1	small red cabbage, coarsely shredded (6–8 cups/1.5–2 L)
1	1	apple, cut into cubes
1½ cups	375 mL	beef broth
½ cup	125 mL	red wine, cooking wine or apple juice
1	1	bay leaf
2	2	peppercorns, crushed
2	2	whole cloves
4–6	4–6	sprigs fresh rosemary (or 2 tsp/10 mL crumbled dried rosemary)

Season roast with salt and pepper; brown on all sides in lightly oiled roasting pan. Add vegetables, apple, broth, wine, bay leaf, peppercorns and cloves to pan. Place fresh rosemary sprigs on roast or add dried rosemary to broth mixture. Cover and simmer on top of stove or cook in 325°F (160°C) oven for approx 3 hours, or until tender.

TIP: To reduce cooking time when using stovetop method, add 1 cup (250 mL) water and increase heat to medium. Cover and cook for about 2 hours, or until tender.

Nutrition Per Serving
270 Calories, 9.5 g Fat, 31 g Protein, 14 g Carbohydrates.
A good source of Iron (22% RDI) and an
excellent source of Zinc (82% RDI)

Ruby-Glazed Roast Beef

Simplify preparation and clean-up with special cellophane-like "oven bags."

Servings: 8–10
Preparation: 10 minutes
Cooking: 1–1½ hours

1 jar	250 mL	red currant jelly
1	1	green onion, minced
¼ cup	50 mL	soy sauce
1 tsp	5 mL	ground ginger
3 lbs	1.5 kg	pot roast or oven roast (blade, cross rib, round or sirloin tip), trimmed of external fat

Preheat oven to 350°F (180°C). Follow instructions on package of regular oven bags. Combine first 4 ingredients. Place roast in bag and pour jelly mixture over meat. Insert meat thermometer through bag into centre of roast. Cook roast in oven bag placed in roaster for approx. 18–21 min/lb (36-42 min/kg) for rare (140°F/60°C on meat thermometer), 21-23 min/lb (42–46 min/kg) for medium (160°F/71°C) and 23–28 min/lb (46–56 min/kg) for well done (170°F/75°C). Slit bag open and remove roast. Slice thinly across the grain and serve drizzled with juices from roast. If desired, juices may be thickened with mixture of 2 tbsp (30 mL) each of cornstarch and cold water.

TIP: If you don't have an "oven bag," brown roast on all sides in a large lightly oiled pot. Add remaining ingredients and cook covered for at least 3 hours on stove top or in a 325°F (160°C) oven.

Nutrition Per Serving

296 Calories, 8.6 g Fat, 24 g Protein, 31 g Carbohydrates

Rush-Hour Roast Beef Dinner

Quick Roasts weighing 1 lb (500 g) or less are just the right size for small families.

Servings: 4
Preparation: 10 minutes
Cooking: 50–60 minutes

1 lb	500 g	beef quick roast (eye of round, inside round or sirloin tip)
1 tbsp	15 mL	packaged onion and roasted garlic soup mix
4 cups	1 L	root vegetables (parsnip, sweet potato or onion), cut into halves

Remove netting from roast; rub with soup mix. Insert meat thermometer lengthwise into centre of roast so that shaft is not visible. Place into shallow ovenproof pan, on bed of root vegetables that have been coated lightly with cooking spray and seasoned. Cook, uncovered, in 350°F (180°C) oven for 50–60 minutes until thermometer reads 155°F (68°C) for medium. Remove roast to cutting board; tent with foil for 5 min to allow temperature to rise 5°F (3°C). Cut into thin slices across the grain and serve with the roasted vegetables.

Nutrition Per Serving
245 Calories, 6 g Fat, 24 g Protein, 24 g Carbohydrates.
A good source of Iron (16 % RDI) and
an excellent source of Zinc (42 % RDI)

Savoury Sunday Roast

This delicious roast provides a comforting dinner, plus many easy weekday meals.

Servings: 12–15
Preparartion: 5 minutes
Cooking: 1¾–2¼ hours

4–5 lb	1.8–2.2 kg	oven roast (inside round, outside round, rump or sirloin tip)
1 tbsp	15 mL	minced garlic (3 cloves) or (1 tsp/5 mL) garlic powder
1 tbsp	15 mL	coarsely ground pepper

Place roast fat side up on rack in roasting pan without lid. Rub with garlic cloves and sprinkle with pepper or use variations below. Insert meat thermometer into center of roast. Add 1½ cups (375 mL) water to pan and place roast in preheated 500°F (260°C) oven. After 30 minutes, reduce oven temperature to 275°F (140°C). Cook an additional 1¼ to 1¾ hours until medium done (i.e., until internal temperature 160°F/71°C).

TIP: *Barbecue Roast*: Combine ¼ cup (50 mL) each strong coffee and your favourite barbecue sauce with 1 tsp (5 mL) minced garlic; brush on roast before and during roasting.
Teriyaki Roast: Combine ¼ cup (50 mL) each sherry and soy sauce with 1 tbsp (15 mL) dry mustard; brush on roast before and during roasting.
Cranberry Roast: Combine 1 can jellied cranberry sauce, 2 chopped green onions, ¼ cup (50 mL) soy sauce, 1 tsp (5 mL) ginger. Heat and spread on roast. Reserve extra and serve heated with roast.

Nutrition Per Serving

109 Calories, 4.3 g Fat, 16 g Protein, 0 g Carbohydrates

Stuffed Cranberry Roast

Impress your guests during the holidays with this easy-to-do stuffed beef roast.

Servings: 8
Preparation: 20 minutes
Cooking: 1¾ hours

3 lb	1.5 kg	oven roast (eye of round)
		ground savory
1	1	box (120 g) seasoned stuffing mix
½ cup	125 mL	melted butter/margarine
1	1	can (14 oz/398 mL) whole cranberry sauce
½ cup	125 mL	grated orange rind (of 2 large oranges)

Combine stuffing mix with melted butter/margarine. Add one-half of the cranberry sauce and orange rind, mixing gently. Cut roast in half lengthways from the topside to within ½ inch (1 cm) of bottom to prepare a V-shaped cavity for stuffing. Sprinkle outside of roast and cavity with savory. Mound cavity with stuffing. Tie each end of roast with string. Place roast, fat side up, on rack in roasting pan, containing water ½ inch (1 cm) deep. Insert meat thermometer into middle of stuffing. Roast uncovered, in a preheated 500°F (260°C) oven for 30 minutes. Heat remaining cranberry sauce and orange rind in a small saucepan, stirring over low heat. Spread sauce over the roast. Roast uncovered at 275ºF (140°C) for an additional 1¼ hours or until the meat thermometer registers 160°F (71°C) for medium. Let stand for a few minutes before carving in 1 inch (2.5 cm) thick slices.

Nutrition Per Serving
536 Calories, 24 g Fat, 40 g Protein, 39 g Carbohydrates.
An excellent source of Iron (34% RDI) and Zinc (64% RDI)

Surf & Turf Beef Roast

Effortless entertaining with decadent results.

Servings: 5–6
Preparation: 15–20 minutes
Cooking: 45–60 minutes

2 (4 oz)	2 (125 g)	lobster tails
2½–3 lbs	1.2–1.5 kg	premium oven roast (whole beef tenderloin)
		Lemon pepper
½ cup	125 mL	melted butter
2 tsp	10 mL	minced garlic
¼ cup	50 mL	chopped green onion
1 cup	250 mL	fresh or canned sliced mushrooms (optional)
½ cup	125 mL	white or red wine (or the juice of 1 lemon)

Preheat oven to 400°F (200°C). Cook lobster tails in boiling, salted water for 5 minutes if fresh/7 minutes if frozen. Drain and rinse with cold water. Meanwhile, cut a lengthwise slit in the tenderloin to within ½-inch (1 cm) from the bottom and spread it open. Fold small pointed end of roast (if there is one) in on itself to make roast an even shape. Sprinkle with lemon pepper. Remove and discard shells and place lobster tails end-to-end down center of beef. Combine butter and garlic and drizzle 2 tbsp (30 mL) over the lobster. Wrap beef around lobster and tie with cooking twine at about 1-inch (2.5 cm) intervals. Place lobster-stuffed roast on rack in roasting pan and sprinkle with lemon pepper. Roast uncovered at 400°F (200°C) for approx 45–60 minutes, until meat thermometer reads 140°F (60°C) for rare to 150°F (65°C) for medium-rare, or to desired doneness. Meanwhile, sauté green onions (and mushrooms, if desired) in remaining garlic butter until golden. Add wine or lemon juice and heat thoroughly. Let roast stand tented with foil for a few minutes before carving into thick slices and serving with wine butter sauce. Serve with assorted steamed vegetables.

Nutrition Per Serving
470 Calories, 29 g Fat, 47 g Protein, 1.1 g Carbohydrates.
An excellent source of Iron (41% RDI) and Zinc (101% RDI)

Tangy Oktoberfest Roast

This one pot meal is juicy and tender with a flavour that everyone will love.

Servings: 8
Preparation: 15 minutes
Cooking: 3 hours

3 lb	1.5 kg	pot roast (brisket or blade)
2 tbsp	30 mL	each: Dijon mustard and brown sugar
2	2	cloves garlic, crushed
¼ tsp	1 mL	nutmeg
3	3	large onions, sliced
1 cup	250 mL	each: beer or ale and beef stock
6	6	carrots, peeled and quartered
3	3	parsnips, peeled and quartered
6–8	6–8	medium new potatoes

Place roast in oven-proof dish. Combine next 4 ingredients in a small bowl, spread mixture over roast and layer with onions. Pour beer and stock over top and season with salt and pepper. Cover and place in preheated oven at 325°F (170°C) for 1½ hours. Add vegetables around beef and cook covered for another 1½ hours, removing lid for last 20–30 minutes to brown roast. Remove beef and vegetables to serving platter and thicken juices with 1 tbsp (15 mL) cornstarch blended with cold water. Bring to a boil, stirring to thicken and serve over roast.

TIP: A dark beer (ale) will give a richer flavour. Parsnips may be replaced by turnip.

Nutrition Per Serving

467 Calories, 17 g Fat, 31 g Protein, 49 g Carbohydrates

Tex-Mex Ribs

If you're craving ribs, you don't have to move to Texas to enjoy good ribs!

Servings: 4
Preparation: 1¼ hours
Cooking: 10–20 minutes
Marinating: 2 hours or overnight

2 lbs	1 kg	boneless beef simmering short ribs (if bone-in, use 3 lbs/ 1.5 kg) or brisket pot roast, trimmed of fat and cut in 2 x 4 inch (5 x 10 cm) pieces
1	1	bottle (200 mL) Tex-Mex style or regular steak sauce
¼ cup	50 mL	extra strong coffee
¼ cup	50 mL	liquid honey
2 tbsp	30 mL	vinegar
1 tbsp	15 mL	Dijon or regular mustard
2 tbsp	30 mL	finely chopped onion
4	4	cloves garlic, crushed

Place ribs in saucepan, add enough water to barely cover ribs (a whole onion and a garlic clove may be added for extra flavour). Bring ribs to a boil, reduce to simmer. Cover and cook 60 minutes, drain ribs. In a small bowl, combine remaining ingredients to make sauce. Marinate cooked ribs in sauce in refrigerator for 2 hours or overnight for extra flavour. Place ribs on broiler pan on second shelf under preheated broiler (or grill about 3 inches [7 cm] above medium heat); brush generously with sauce. Broil/grill for about 10–20 minutes until browned, brushing with sauce often and turning frequently. Heat any remaining sauce to the boil (add water if sauce is too thick) and simmer for 5 minutes to serve as a dipping sauce.

TIP: This recipe may be made in a 4-quart (4 L) slow cooker by combining all ingredients with ½ cup (125 mL) water. Cover and cook on High for 4–5 hours (or on Low for 8–10 hours). Skim off fat and remove bones, if any.

Nutrition Per Serving

431 Calories, 20 g Fat, 40 g Protein, 21 g Carbohydrates

Asian Hot Pot

For a fun party, or family dinner, try this lighter version of beef fondue.

Servings: 4
Cooking: 15 minutes

5 cups	1.25 L	beef broth
1 tbsp	15 mL	soy sauce
2–3 tsp	10–15 mL	minced ginger root
2	2	cloves garlic, minced
3 tbsp	45 mL	chopped fresh coriander or cilantro
3	3	green onions, sliced
1 lb	500 g	beef fondue cubes or grilling steak (top sirloin, rib eye, rib, tenderloin or striploin) cut into ¾-inch cubes
4 cups	1 L	broccoli or cauliflower florets, mushrooms, red pepper chunks or zucchini cubes
Soup:		
2 cups	500 mL	coarsely shredded spinach
1 oz	30 g	thin rice vermicelli or fine noodles, broken (about 1 cup/ 250 mL)
Dipping Sauces:		peanut, honey garlic, teriyaki or soy (optional)

In a fondue pot, hot pot or small wok combine first 6 ingredients; bring to a boil and heat 5 minutes. Arrange beef cubes and vegetable pieces on separate platters; set on table near fondue pot allowing everyone to cook their own in the boiling broth with fondue forks, dipping in sauces if desired. When everyone has finished be sure there are about 4 cups broth left in fondue pot, if not add some water or broth; add spinach and noodles. Season with additional green onions and coriander, if desired. Boil 5 minutes or until noodles are tender. Serve in individual soup bowls.

Nutrition Per Serving

233 Calories, 5.8 g Fat, 32 g Protein, 13 g Carbohydrates

Autumn Steak with Mulling Spices

Here's a recipe that embraces the flavours of the harvest and the tradition of pickling.

Servings: 4
Preparation: 15 minutes
Cooking: 1¼ hours

1 tsp	5 mL	vegetable oil
1 lb	500 g	simmering steak (blade or cross rib), cut into 4 equal pieces
		Salt and pepper
1	1	can (28 oz/796 mL) diced tomatoes
1	1	small white onion, thinly sliced into rings
1	1	small green pepper, cut into strips
2	2	stalks celery, chopped
¼ cup	50 mL	each: vinegar and ketchup
2 tbsp	30 mL	packed brown sugar
¼ tsp	1 mL	ground cinnamon
⅛ tsp	½ mL	ground cloves
2 tsp	10 mL	cornstarch

In a Dutch oven or stockpot, heat oil over medium-high heat. Season steaks with salt and pepper and brown on both sides. Combine remaining ingredients, except cornstarch; pour over steak. Simmer, covered on stove top or in a 325°F (160°C) oven for 1¼ hours or until fork tender. Remove steak from pan and set aside. In small cup, mix cornstarch with 1 tbsp (15 mL) cold water until smooth. Heat sauce on stovetop over medium heat. Gradually stir in cornstarch mixture; stir and boil for 1 to 2 minutes or until thickened. Season to taste. Return steak to pan. Serve with rice, couscous or mashed potatoes.

Nutrition Per Serving
273 Calories, 8 g Fat, 26 g Protein, 26 g Carbohydrates.
An excellent source of Iron (30% RDI) and Zinc (88% RDI)

Balsamic-Beer Flank Steak

A great steak which can also be sliced into a salad with the hot marinade sauce.

Servings: 6
Preparation: 15 minutes
Cooking: 10–12 minutes
Marinating: 12–24 hours

1 ½ lbs	750 g	marinating steak (flank, inside round, outside round, sirloin tip)
½ cup	125 mL	beer (either ale or lager) or sherry
1	1	small onion, finely chopped
2	2	cloves garlic, minced
¼ cup	50 mL	ketchup
1 tbsp	15 mL	chili powder
2 tbsp	30 mL	balsamic vinegar
2 tbsp	30 mL	brown sugar
4 tsp	20 mL	grainy or Dijon mustard
½ tsp	2 mL	each: salt and pepper

Pierce steak several times with fork; place in resealable plastic bag or in shallow dish. Combine remaining ingredients; mix well and pour over meat. Seal bag tightly or cover dish. Let meat marinate in refrigerator, turning occasionally, for at least 12 hours. Remove meat from marinade and grill over medium-high heat for 5–6 minutes on each side for medium doneness; remove from heat and allow to rest 5 minutes. Transfer marinade to small saucepan and boil for 5–10 minutes until slightly thickened. To serve, slice steak in thin strips across the grain and top with sauce, if desired.

TIP: To speed up this recipe, combine the contents of one 20–40 g pouch of quick marinade for beef (usually sold at the meat case of most stores) with the recipe ingredients listed above. Marinate the steak for 30 minutes in the mixture and then cook as above.

Nutrition Per Serving
234 Calories, 8.7 g Fat, 26 g Protein, 12 g Carbohydrates.
A good source of Iron (16% RDI) and an
excellent source of Zinc (64% RDI)

BBQ Flank Steak "Parisienne"

An easy open-face sandwich variation of the French classic bagette à l'échalotte.

Servings: 8
Preparation: 20 minutes
Cooking: 12–15 minutes
Marinating: 12 hours

1 cup	250 mL	red wine
1	1	shallot, minced
2	2	garlic cloves, crushed
1	1	sprig of fresh thyme (or ½ tsp/2 mL dried)
1	1	bay leaf
		Salt and fresh ground pepper to taste
1½ lb	750 g	marinating steak (flank, inside or outside round)
2	2	French baguettes (14 inches/35 cm long), cut in half lengthwise
½ cup	125 mL	Dijon mustard
4 oz	115 g	Brie cheese, thinly sliced
¼ cup	50 mL	broken walnut pieces, optional

To prepare marinade: Combine red wine, shallot, garlic, thyme, bay leaf, salt and pepper in large resealable freezer bag. Pierce steak numerous times with fork. Add steak to bag; seal tightly and refrigerate for 12 hours. Remove steak from bag and reserve marinade. Pat steak dry; place on preheated greased grill and sear on both sides. Reduce heat to medium; close lid and cook steak, turning once, for about 5–6 minutes per side (best cooked only to medium). Remove steak from heat; let sit for 10 minutes. Meanwhile, boil reserved marinade for 5–7 minutes; discard thyme sprig and bay leaf. For optimum tenderness, slice steak as thinly as possible, on a 45-degree angle to the cutting board. To make sandwiches, cut baguette halves in two and spread with mustard, top with sliced steak and cheese. Grill baguettes just until cheese melts. Sprinkle with walnut pieces, if desired. Serve immediately with heated marinade and grilled tomatoes and pommes frites, if desired.

Nutrition Per Serving

411 Calories, 14 g Fat, 30 g Protein, 38 g Carbohydrates.
An excellent source of Iron (26% RDI) and Zinc (60% RDI)

BBQ Steak with Saucy Mushrooms

Cook onions with mushrooms or add cooked bacon pieces for additional flavour.

Servings: 4
Preparation: 5 minutes
Cooking: 10–22 minutes

1 lb	500 g	grilling steaks (top sirloin, rib eye, strip loin or tenderloin), cut ¾–1-inch (2–2.5 cm) thick
1 tsp	5 mL	packaged steak seasoning
½ lb	250 g	mushrooms, sliced
¼ cup	50 mL	green pepper, diced
½ cup	125 mL	bottled BBQ Sauce

Sprinkle and press steak seasoning on both sides of steak. Grill or broil steak according to chart. Meanwhile in medium skillet, heat 1 tbsp (15 mL) vegetable oil over medium-high heat; cook and stir mushrooms 3–4 minutes or until lightly browned. Stir in green pepper and BBQ sauce and heat until warm. Serve mushrooms with steak, baked potatoes and corn.

TIP: Mix leftover steak or roast beef strips, cooked onions or mushrooms with BBQ sauce and heat to warm; wrap in warm tortillas or spoon onto hamburger buns.

Nutrition Per Serving

168 Calories, 5.5 g Fat, 23 g Protein, 6 g Carbohydrates

Beef and Orange Kabobs

A sweet, medium spiced beef dish with an exotic flare.

Servings: 4
Preparation: 20 minutes
Cooking: 10–15 minutes

1	1	navel orange
1	1	container (175 g) plain yogurt
1 tbsp	15 mL	bottled Madras paste
1 lb	500 g	beef grilling kabobs (top sirloin or strip loin), cut in 1½-inch cubes
1	1	green pepper, seeds removed and cut into chunks
3	3	onions, quartered

Grate ½ tsp (2 mL) rind from the orange, then peel it. Slice the orange across the segments to give wheel shapes. Mix together the orange rind, yogurt and the bottled Madras curry paste. Set aside 2–3 tbsp (30–45 mL) of yogurt mixture in a small dish. Place the beef cubes into the remaining yogurt mixture, stir and refrigerate for 10 minutes. Thread the steak, pepper, onion and orange alternately onto skewers and grill or broil for 10–15 minutes, turning occasionally and basting with the yogurt set aside earlier. Serve on a bed of rice or with salad.

Nutrition Per Serving

224 Calories, 7.4 g Fat, 24 g Protein, 15 g Carbohydrates

Bombay Beef & Cauliflower

Try chilling before serving, or adjust the "heat" by using mild curry powder.

Servings: 4
Cooking: 30–35 minutes

⅔ cup	150 mL	plain low-fat yogurt
1 tbsp	15 mL	cornstarch
2 tsp	10 mL	curry powder
¼ cup	50 mL	honey mustard
1 lb	500 g	top sirloin grilling steak, cut into ½ inch (1 cm) cubes
4 cups	1 L	small cauliflower florets (approx. 1 head cauliflower)
1	1	can (10 oz/289 mL) beef broth
1	1	package (250 g) snow peas, defrosted
4 cups	1 L	hot cooked fusilli (or other pasta, couscous or rice)
¼ cup	50 mL	toasted slivered almonds (optional)

Combine first 4 ingredients and pepper to taste in a small bowl; stir well with a whisk and set aside. Heat a large, oiled, non-stick skillet over high heat. Add meat and sauté 3 minutes or until browned. Remove from skillet and set aside. Add cauliflower and broth; cover, reduce heat and simmer 3 minutes. Return meat to skillet; stir in yogurt mixture. Add snow peas and bring to a boil; cook 2 minutes, stirring gently. Toss with pasta before serving. Garnish with toasted almonds, if desired. Good served cold as a luncheon salad.

Nutrition Per Serving

455 Calories, 9 g Fat, 39 g Protein, 54 g Carbohydrates

Brewed Beef with Roasted Root Vegetables

The aroma of this hearty, beer-simmered steak is a warm welcome on a cool evening.

Servings: 4
Preparation: 35 minutes
Cooking: 1¼ hours

2	2	slices bacon, finely diced
1 lb	500 g	simmering steak (blade or cross rib), cut into 4 equal pieces
		Salt and pepper
2	2	garlic cloves, minced
4	4	medium onions, thinly sliced
2 tbsp	50 mL	all-purpose flour
2 tsp	10 mL	white wine vinegar
½ tsp	2 mL	granulated sugar
1 tsp	5 mL	thyme
1	1	can (284 mL) undiluted beef broth
1	1	bottle (341 mL) beer
2	2	bay leaves
		serve with Roasted Root Vegetables (see below)

Cook bacon in a Dutch oven or stockpot over medium-high heat until crisp; remove bacon and set aside. Season steak with salt and pepper and brown on both sides in bacon drippings. Remove from pan. Add garlic and onions to pan; cover and cook over medium heat for 10 minutes, stirring occasionally. Stir in flour and cook for 1 minute. Add remaining ingredients and bring to a simmer. Return bacon and steak to pan; cover and cook in 325°F (160°C) oven for 1¼ hours or until fork tender. *Roasted Root Vegetables*: cut 2 carrots and parsnips and ½ red and green peppers into 1 in (2.5 cm) pieces. Combine with 1 cup (250 mL) each 1 in/2.5 cm cubes butternut squash and sweet potato. Toss vegetables with 1 tbsp (15 mL) each balsamic vinegar, olive oil, chopped fresh rosemary leaves and 1 tsp (5 mL) granulated sugar. Oven roast in a single layer on baking sheet at 325°F (160°C) while meat cooks.

Nutrition Per Serving
309 Calories, 14 g Fat, 28 g Protein, 17 g Carbohydrates.
A good source of Iron (24% RDI) and an
excellent source of Zinc (87% RDI)

Cheese Crowned Tenderloins

Your answer for an elegant meal that doesn't take hours to prepare.

Servings: 4
Preparation: 2 minutes
Cooking: 10 minutes

4	4	4 oz/125 mL grilling steaks (beef tenderloin or top sirloin)
¼ cup	50 mL	herbed chèvre or cream cheese
½ cup	125 mL	seedless raspberry jam
¼ cup	50 mL	balsamic vinegar

In medium, oiled skillet over medium-high heat, brown steaks 3–4 minutes on each side. Remove to baking pan and top each steak with one quarter of the cheese. Broil 3 minutes or until cheese is browned. Meanwhile stir jam and vinegar into skillet and bring just to boil. Serve steaks on a pool of sauce, drizzling a little over top. Variation: Substitute whole cranberry sauce for jam and dry red wine for vinegar

TIP: Simply halve the recipe for a candlelight dinner for two.

Nutrition Per Serving

321 Calories, 13 g Fat, 21 g Protein, 31 g Carbohydrates.
An excellent source of Iron (39% RDI) and Zinc (45% RDI)

Mustard Medallions with Sage Onion Compote   page 114

Flaming Fajitas   page 103

Beef Bourguignon page 132

BBQ Flank Steak "Parisienne" page 91

Involtini of Sirloin Steak   page 105

Grilled Beef Tenderloin with Goat Cheese page 104

Rosemary Pot Roast with Braised Vegetables page 80

Homestyle Beef Stew   *page 136*

Cinnamon Braised Beef

The wonderful aroma will whet your appetite!

Servings: 4
Preparation: 15 minutes
Cooking: 1¼ hours

1 tsp	5 mL	vegetable oil
1 lb	500 g	simmering steak (blade or cross rib) cut into 4 equal pieces
½ cup	125 mL	sake (rice wine)
2 tbsp	30 mL	soy sauce
1 tbsp	15 mL	granulated sugar
2	2	green onions, cut into 1-inch (2.5 cm) pieces
2	2	garlic cloves, crushed
2	2	cinnamon sticks, 4 inches (10 cm) in length
1	1	piece (1 inch/2.5 cm) fresh ginger root, sliced
2 tsp	10 mL	cornstarch
5 oz	125 g	spinach, chopped

In a Dutch oven or stockpot, heat oil over medium-high heat, and brown steaks on both sides. Add 1½ cups (375 mL) water; combine remaining ingredients except cornstarch and spinach and pour over steak. Simmer, covered, on stove-top or in a 325°F (160°C) oven for 1¼ hours or until fork-tender. Remove cinnamon sticks and ginger; discard. Remove steak and set aside. Heat sauce over medium heat on stove-top. Meanwhile, in small cup, mix cornstarch with 1 tbsp (15 mL) cold water until smooth. Gradually stir into sauce and bring to a boil; heat and stir for 1 to 2 minutes, until thickened. Season to taste. Return steak to pan. Stir in spinach and cook for 3 minutes until wilted. Serve with cooked Chinese noodles or vermicelli.

TIP: Can be made in a slow cooker; combine all ingredients except cornstarch and spinach and cook covered for 5 hours on high or 8 hours on low until meat is fork-tender. Thicken sauce on stove-top as above. Add spinach and cook for 3 minutes or until wilted.

Nutrition Per Serving

212 Calories, 8 g Fat, 25 g Protein, 8 g Carbohydrates.
An excellent source of Iron (29% RDI) and Zinc (87% RDI)

Creole Mustard Beef Oscar

Surf and turf at it's best!

Servings: 4
Cooking: 30 minutes

½ lb	250 g	combination of: fresh or frozen shrimp, lobster claws and/or scallops
8 spears	8 spears	fresh or frozen asparagus, cut in 2-inch (5 cm) pieces
1 lb	500 g	grilling steaks (beef strip loin or rib eye)
1 tsp	5 mL	minced garlic
½ bottle	175 mL	bottled Creole mustard sauce
½ tsp	2 mL	dried parsley or tarragon
		Freshly grated black pepper
2 tbsp	30 mL	Parmesan cheese (optional)

Cook seafood and asparagus in boiling, salted water for 2–3 minutes. Drain. Season steaks with favourite steak spice and broil, grill or pan-fry to desired doneness (approx 3–4 minutes per side). Meanwhile, add garlic to a lightly oiled frying pan and sauté. Stir in Creole mustard sauce, parsley, pepper, cooked seafood and asparagus and heat through. Pour entire contents of pan over cooked steaks. Sprinkle with freshly grated Parmesan, if desired.

Nutrition Per Serving
352 Calories, 15 g Fat, 37 g Protein, 15 g Carbohydrates.
A good source of Iron (19% RDI) and an
excellent source of Zinc (66% RDI)

Easy Asian Steak

This simple dish allows the meat to marinate, tenderize and cook all at once.

Servings: 4
Preparation: 5 minutes
Cooking: 1¼ hours

1½ tsp	7 mL	vegetable oil
1 lb	500 g	simmering steak (blade or cross rib)
¾ cup	175 mL	orange juice
3 tbsp	45 mL	each: soy sauce and ketchup
1½ tbsp	22 mL	ginger root, grated
¼ tsp	1 mL	dried chili peppers
1½ tsp	7 mL	cornstarch

In medium oven-proof skillet (wrap skillet handle in foil if not oven-proof) heat oil over medium-high heat; brown steak, about 2 minutes on each side. Meanwhile, mix remaining ingredients except cornstarch; pour over steak. Remove from heat; cover and simmer in 325°F (180°C) oven for 1¼ hours or until tender. Remove steak to cutting board; place skillet over medium heat; mix cornstarch with 1 tbsp (15 mL) water until smooth, stir into skillet and bring to boil for 1 minute. Slice steak in thin strips. Serve over rice or Chinese noodles or fettuccini. Toss noodles with sauce and top with steak. Garnish with grated orange rind, sliced green onions and/or fresh coriander (optional).

TIP: For a more exotic flavour, substitute fish sauce for soy; vary the chili peppers to taste.

Nutrition Per Serving

187 Calories, 8.0 g Fat, 18 g Protein, 11 g Carbohydrates

English Pub-Style Beef

This warm and wonderful meal is done in minutes for a quick comfort food.

Servings: 4
Preparation: 10 minutes
Cooking: 10 minutes

1 lb	500 g	grilling steak (top sirloin or strip loin), cut into strips
1	1	can (10oz/284 mL) tomato soup
2 tbsp	30 mL	Worcestershire sauce
1 tsp	5 mL	sugar
1	1	green and/or yellow pepper, cut into strips
½ lb	250 g	sliced mushrooms

In a large, lightly oiled skillet, stir-fry steak strips for about 2 minutes until no longer pink. Remove from pan. Combine remaining ingredients in skillet and cook over medium-high heat for 5 minutes, stirring occasionally. Stir in beef and heat through. Serve over mashed potatoes, cooked rice, noodles or warm tea biscuits.

Nutrition Per Serving

222 Calories, 5.8 g Fat, 27 g Protein, 16 g Carbohydrates

Fantastic Beef Fajitas

Ideal for casual get togethers.

Servings: 4
Preparation: 10 minutes
Cooking: 2–3 minutes
Marinating: 10–15 minutes

1	1	lime (grated peel and juice)
2 tbsp	30 mL	orange juice
2 tsp	10 mL	minced garlic (2 cloves) or 1 tsp (5 mL) garlic powder
2 tbsp	30 mL	mild or medium chutney
½ tsp	2 mL	cumin
1 lb	500 g	beef stir-fry strips or marinating steak (inside round, outside round or sirloin tip), cut in strips
8	8	flour tortillas (6-inch/15 cm diameter) or flavoured wraps
½ cup	125 mL	shredded cheddar cheese
½ cup	125 mL	guacamole or sour cream

In a shallow dish, combine peel, juices, garlic, chutney and cumin. Add beef strips, cover and marinate for 10–15 minutes. Meanwhile, wrap tortillas in foil and place in non-stick frypan over medium heat for 5 minutes, turning once. Remove from pan and turn heat to high. Drain beef strips, stir-fry 2–3 minutes. Top warmed tortillas with beef strips, cheese and guacamole or sour cream and fold up. Serve with spinach and orange salad.

TIP: For serving ease, set out a variety of toppings and wraps and let each person build their own fajitas.

Nutrition Per Serving

392 Calories, 15 g Fat, 34 g Protein, 31 g Carbohydrates.
An excellent source of Iron (38% RDI) and Zinc (54% RDI)

Fettucine with Roasted Red Pepper & Garlic Cream Sauce

Exquisite flavour for those special occasions.

Servings: 4–6
Cooking: 20–25 minutes

½ box	450 g	fettucine
1 lb	500 g	grilling steak (top sirloin or strip loin) cut in stir-fry strips
1 tsp	5 mL	minced garlic
		Freshly ground black pepper, to taste
1 bottle	350 mL	bottled light roasted red pepper and garlic dressing
1 cup	250 mL	light sour cream
1 tsp	5 mL	sugar
1 lb	500 g	fresh or frozen asparagus spears, cut in 2-inch (5 cm) pieces
1	1	can (7 oz/199 mL) sweet red pimientos
¼ cup	50 mL	pine nuts

Prepare fettucine according to package directions. Meanwhile, stir-fry beef strips with garlic and pepper in lightly oiled non-stick frypan for 2–3 minutes, until no longer pink. Remove beef to plate using slotted spoon. Combine bottled roasted red pepper and garlic dressing with sour cream and sugar in pan with meat juices. Add asparagus to pan with sauce, cover and simmer for 2–3 minutes. Drain fettucine and add with cooked beef strips and pimientos to sauce. Mix well and heat through. Serve sprinkled with pine nuts.

Nutrition Per Serving
527 Calories, 13 g Fat, 32 g Protein, 70 g Carbohydrates.
An excellent source of Iron (34% RDI) and Zinc (52% RDI)

Flaming Fajitas

By grilling everything, this entire meal is cooked in the great outdoors.

Servings: 4
Preparation: 15 minutes
Cooking: 11 minutes
Marinating: 8–12 hours

1	1	lime
½ cup	125 mL	finely chopped pickled jalapeno peppers plus 2 tbsp (30 mL) reserved juice
2 tbsp	30 mL	Worcestershire sauce
2	2	garlic cloves, minced
1 lb	500 g	marinating steak (flank, inside or outside round, or sirloin tip), ¾-inch (2 cm) thick
1	1	each onion and sweet red pepper, cut into strips
1 tbsp	15 mL	vegetable oil
1 tsp	5 mL	chili powder
½ tsp	2 mL	ground cumin
4	4	Greek pitas

Combine finely grated peel and juice from lime, jalapenos and their reserved juice, Worcestershire sauce and half the garlic in large sealable freezer bag. Pierce beef all over with fork and add to bag; refrigerate 8–12 hours. Discard marinade; grill steak using medium-high heat, 3–4 minutes/side for rare. Let stand for 5 minutes; slice thinly across the grain. Meanwhile, toss vegetables with oil, remaining garlic and seasonings; grill in grilling basket using medium-high heat for 5 minutes, stirring occasionally. Tuck steak and vegetables into warm pitas and top with some salsa.

TIP: When using a grilling steak, like top sirloin, reduce the marinating time to 30–60 minutes.

Nutrition Per Serving

354 Calories, 8 g Fat, 31 g Protein, 39 g Carbohydrates

Grilled Beef Tenderloin with Goat Cheese

Chopped garlic flowers in oil is a product that imparts a mild sweet garlic flavour.

Servings: 2
Preparation: 10–15 minutes
Cooking: 10–15 minutes

2	2	grilling steaks (tenderloin, top sirloin, rib eye or strip loin) each 8 oz/225 g and 1-inch/2.5 cm thick
1 tbsp	15 mL	balsamic vinegar
½ cup	125 mL	whipping cream
1 tsp	5 mL	chopped garlic flowers in oil (or ½ tsp/2 mL minced garlic)
¼ tsp	1 mL	dried basil leaves (or 1 tsp/5 mL fresh chopped basil)
3 tbsp	45 mL	crumbled fresh goat cheese (e.g., chèvre)
1	1	small fresh tomato, seeded and finely diced
1	1	small green onion, white part only, chopped
1 tsp	5 mL	chopped fresh parsley
		Salt and pepper
		Olive oil

Preheat barbecue to medium-high 400°F (200°C). Brush steaks with vinegar; set aside. In small saucepan, bring cream, chopped garlic flowers in oil and basil to boil; reduce heat to low and simmer until volume reduces by half. Add cheese; stir with wooden spoon until completely blended. Remove from heat. Add diced tomatoes, chopped green onion and parsley to sauce. Season with salt and pepper. Lightly brush steaks with oil and sear both sides on barbecue. Reduce heat to medium; cook 3–5 minutes per side for rare or 5–7 minutes per side for medium, turning meat once. Serve steak with sauce, baked potatoes or rice, sautéed green beans and wild mushrooms, if desired. Garnish with tomato wedge and sprig of parsley or fresh basil.

Nutrition Per Serving

621 Calories, 45 g Fat, 47 g Protein, 6.1 g Carbohydrates

Involtini of Sirloin Steak

Same technique as the classic German beef roulade, but adapted for the barbecue.

Servings: 4–6
Preparation: 20 minutes
Cooking: 10 minutes

1½ lb	750 g	grilling steak (top sirloin) or rouladen-cut inside round marinating steak
		Salt & pepper to taste
4 oz	115 g	peppered goat cheese (e.g., chèvre or feta with black pepper)
2 tsp	10 mL	dried oregano, crumbled
2 cups	500 mL	fresh spinach leaves
12	12	sun-dried tomato pieces (oil-packed)
2 tbsp	30 mL	balsamic vinegar
		Olive oil

If using sirloin steak, use a mallet to pound steak to ⅛ inch (0.25 cm) thickness (this step is not necessary if using rouladen-cut steaks). Season beef with salt and pepper. Spread goat cheese to within ¼ inch (0.5 cm) of each steak's edge; sprinkle with oregano. Place half of the spinach leaves over cheese. Add sun-dried tomatoes and cover completely with remaining spinach. Starting with long edge, roll up each steak like a jelly roll. Tie tightly in several places with butcher's twine or hold together with skewers (presoak wooden skewers for 1 hour). Brush outside of each beef roll with balsamic vinegar and olive oil; season with salt and pepper. Place beef on greased grill over medium heat; close lid and cook, turning once, for approximately 3–5 minutes per side (until instant-read thermometer inserted into center of each roll reads 155°F/68°C). Remove from heat; place seam-side-down on cutting board and tent with foil for 5 minutes. Remove string or skewers and cut diagonally into 1-inch (2.5-cm) slices. Serve the involtini with new potatoes and grilled vegetables tossed in a balsamic vinaigrette.

Nutrition Per Serving
248 Calories, 12 g Fat, 30 g Protein, 4.5 g Carbohydrates.
An excellent source of Iron (28% RDI) and Zinc (58% RDI)

Java Pepper Steak

This rub perks up your steak!

Servings: 4
Preparation: 5 minutes
Cooking: 10–12 minutes

1½ lbs	750 g	4 grilling steaks (rib eye, strip loin, top sirloin or tenderloin)
4 tsp	20 mL	finely ground coffee (optional)
4 tsp	20 mL	freshly ground black pepper
2 tsp	10 mL	ground cumin
		Salt to taste

Preheat barbecue or broiler. Meanwhile, combine coffee, pepper, cumin and salt in large resealable freezer bag. Shake each steak separately in bag until evenly coated. Grill, broil or pan-fry steaks for 5–6 minutes per side or until cooked to desired doneness.

TIP: The coffee in this recipe beautifully balances out the other flavours; however, if you think it's too unusual, it can be omitted.

Nutrition Per Serving

284 Calories, 12 g Fat, 40 g Protein, 2.2 g Carbohydrates

Key Lime Steaks

This tangy marinade adds the perfect flavour to your steaks.

Servings: 4
Preparation: 5 minutes
Cooking: 10–20 minutes
Marinating: 12 to 24 hours

1.5 lbs	750 g	marinating or grilling steak (inside or outside round, rib eye, sirloin tip, strip loin or tenderloin)
2 tbsp	30 mL	each: soy sauce and honey
½ tsp	2 mL	Tabasco sauce
¼ cup	50 mL	lime juice
1 tsp	5 mL	ground cumin
2 tbsp	30 mL	oyster sauce (optional)

Combine all ingredients except steaks in a freezer bag and massage to mix. Remove ¼ cup (50 mL) of the marinade and set aside. Add steaks to freezer bag and marinate in remaining mixture in the refrigerator 12–24 hours for marinating steaks, 10–15 minutes for grilling steaks. Grill or broil steaks, turning only once or twice according to desired doneness, basting with reserved marinade while grilling. Marinade ingredients can be doubled if required.

Nutrition Per Serving

254 Calories, 9.1 g Fat, 32 g Protein, 10 g Carbohydrates

Lemon Pepper Steak For Two

When you want something simple yet special, here's the ideal no-fuss supper.

Servings: 2
Cooking: 15 minutes

½ lb	250 g	grilling steak (rib eye, tenderloin, top sirloin or strip loin), cut ¾-inch (2 cm) thick
1 tsp	2 mL	cracked black peppercorns
pinch	pinch	salt
½ tsp	2 mL	butter
⅓ cup	75 mL	beef stock
pinch	pinch	grated lemon rind
2 tsp	10 mL	lemon juice

Trim fat from steak. Press peppercorns onto both sides. Barbecue or broil steak, turning once, for 6 minutes or until browned but rare inside. Transfer to heated plate, sprinkle with salt. Tent with foil; let stand for 5 minutes. Meanwhile, heat butter in a small skillet on medium. Add stock, lemon rind and juice; bring to a boil, stirring for about 2 minutes or until syrupy. Pour in any juices that have accumulated on steak plate. Serve sauce drizzled over steak.

Nutrition Per Serving

185 Calories, 8 g Fat, 27 g Protein, 1 g Carbohydrates

Louis' Cola-Kiwi Steaks

To a great guy who believed everything tasted better when cooked with cola.

Servings: 4
Preparation: 5 minutes
Cooking: 10–12 minutes
Marinating: 30 minutes

1 lb	500 g	marinating steak (round, sirloin tip or flank)
1	1	kiwi, peeled
1 cup	250 mL	cola beverage
1½ tsp	7 mL	lemon pepper

Place kiwi in freezer bag and seal tightly. Mash kiwi to a pulp in bag. Add cola and combine with kiwi by massaging mixture together. Pierce steak numerous times with a fork. Add steak to freezer bag, seal and marinate in refrigerator for 30 minutes (no longer or meat will go mushy), turning bag over once or twice. Meanwhile, preheat barbecue or broiler. Discard marinade. Season steak with lemon pepper and barbecue or broil for 5–6 minutes per side, until it reaches desired doneness.

Nutrition Per Serving

146 Calories, 5 g Fat, 21 g Protein, 2.4 g Carbohydrates

Low-Fat Honey Dijon Marinated Steak

Make extras and use the leftovers in a refreshing salad.

Servings: 6
Preparation: 5 minutes
Cooking: 15 minutes
Marinating: 12 hours

1½ lbs	750 g	marinating steak (inside round, outside round, eye of round, sirloin tip or flank)
¼ cup	50 mL	each: honey Dijon salad dressing and red wine vinegar
2	2	cloves garlic, finely minced
1	1	orange, juice and grated peel

Pierce steak with a fork and place in plastic zipper bag. Combine remaining ingredients and pour over meat. Marinate for at least 12 hours or overnight in refrigerator, turning several times. Remove meat from marinade and broil (or grill on preheated barbecue over medium-high heat) for 5–7 minutes per side for rare, 7–9 minutes per side for medium. Discard marinade. To serve, carve steak in thin slices on the diagonal across the grain.

TIP: A simmering steak (such as blade, cross rib or top blade) would also work well in this recipe.

Nutrition Per Serving

141 Calories, 3.2 g Fat, 25 g Protein, 1.4 g Carbohydrates

Mandarin Orange Pepper Steak

A wonderful blend of flavours in this easy to prepare entree.

Servings: 4
Preparation: 5–10 minutes
Cooking: 10–12 minutes
Marinating: 12–24 hours

1 lb	500 g	marinating steak (flank, inside round, outside round or sirloin tip
¾ cup	200 mL	bottled mandarin orange sauce
½ cup	125 mL	dark beer or stout
1	1	small onion, finely chopped
1 tsp	5 mL	minced garlic
		Cracked black pepper to taste

Pierce steak several times with fork; place in resealable plastic bag or shallow dish. Combine remaining ingredients, except pepper; mix well and pour over meat. Seal bag tightly or cover dish. Let meat marinate in refrigerator, turning occasionally, for at least 12 hours. Remove meat from marinade, season with pepper and broil, grill or pan-fry over medium-high heat for 5 to 6 minutes per side for medium doneness; remove from heat and allow to rest 5 minutes. Transfer marinade to small saucepan and boil for 5–10 minutes, until slightly thickened. To serve, slice steak in thin strips across the grain and top with sauce, if desired. Alternately, place steak slices over rice or orzo pasta and use the hot marinade sauce as dressing.

Nutrition Per Serving
296 Calories, 8.8 g Fat, 26 g Protein, 24 g Carbohydrates.
A source of Iron (13% RDI) and an excellent
source of Zinc (66% RDI)

Middle Eastern Grilled Steak Pockets

Cook the beef only to medium and slice it across the grain, as thin as possible.

Servings: 6
Preparation: 10 minutes
Cooking: 12 minutes
Marinating: 12–24 hours

¼ cup	50 mL	cranberry juice or red wine
3	3	cloves garlic, minced
3 tbsp	45 mL	mild curry paste
2 tbsp	30 mL	each: rice vinegar and olive oil (optional)
1 tsp	5 mL	Worcestershire sauce
1½ lb	750 g	marinating steak (flank, round or sirloin tip)
		Salt and pepper to taste
3	3	pita breads, halved
		Cucumber slices
		Cucumber yogurt sauce, like tzatziki

In large freezer bag, combine cranberry juice, garlic, curry paste, vinegar, oil (if using) and Worcestershire sauce. Pierce steak several times with fork. Add steak to freezer bag, seal tightly and refrigerate, turning occasionally, for 12–24 hours. Preheat grill to medium-high. Discard marinade. Season steak with salt and pepper. Place on greased grill; close lid and cook for 6 minutes per side to medium doneness. Remove from the heat; let stand 5 minutes. Slice steak into thin strips diagonally across the grain. Tuck steak slices into warm pita halves with cucumber slices and yogurt sauce. Serve with rice or couscous salad.

Nutrition Per Serving
286 Calories, 10 g Fat, 28 g Protein, 18 g Carbohydrates

Moroccan Beef with Tabbouleh

Take a trip to Morocco tonight with this tasty combination of flavours and textures.

Servings: 4
Cooking: 35 minutes

1 cup	250 mL	raw pot barley or bulgur
1	1	(¾ oz/21 g) package hot & spicy Szechwan oriental style seasoning mix
1 tsp	5 mL	sugar
3 tbsp	45 mL	soy sauce
1 lb	500 g	marinating steak (flank, round or sirloin tip), sliced into ¼-inch (0.5 cm) thick strips
1 tbsp	15 mL	olive oil
3 tbsp	45 mL	lemon juice
¼ cup	50 mL	each: finely chopped fresh mint, cilantro (coriander) and green onions
¼ tsp	1 mL	each: cumin, lemon pepper and hot pepper sauce (optional)

Bring 2 cups (500 mL) salted water to a boil, add barley or bulgur and simmer covered for 30 minutes. Meanwhile, combine seasoning mix with sugar, soy sauce and ¼ cup (50 mL) water and add steak strips; toss to coat. Just before barley is ready, start stir-frying beef strips in lightly oiled non-stick pan until lightly browned. Remove barley from heat and add olive oil and remaining ingredients. Stir and serve on platter with beef strips over top.

TIP: Leftovers are delicious served cold as a luncheon item.

Nutrition Per Serving

444 Calories, 13 g Fat, 33 g Protein, 48 g Carbohydrates

Mustard Medallions with Sage Onion Compote

A tasty update to the steak and onions classic.

Servings: 2–4
Preparation: 15 minutes
Cooking: 15 minutes
Marinating: 2–24 hours

2 tbsp	30 mL	lemon juice
1 tbsp	15 mL	each: Dijon mustard and olive oil
1	1	clove garlic, minced
1 tsp	5 mL	dried thyme
1 lb	500 g	marinating steak (sirloin tip, outside round or flank), or grilling medallion (top sirloin, strip loin, tenderloin or rib eye), 1 inch (2.5 cm) thick (approx 2 steaks)
		serve with Sage Onion Compote (see below)

In resealable freezer bag, combine lemon juice, mustard, oil, garlic and thyme. Add medallions to bag; seal tightly and refrigerate 12–24 hours for marinating medallions and steaks or 2–4 hours for grilling medallions. Discard marinade. Grill, broil or sauté using medium-high heat, for 6–7 minutes per side for medium doneness. Best cooked only to medium. After grilling slice steak thinly across the grain. Serve steaks with warm Sage Onion Compote.

Sage Onion Compote: In heavy saucepan, heat 2 tbsp (30 mL) butter and 1 tbsp (15 mL) vegetable oil over medium heat. Add 3 cups (750 mL) sliced red onion; cook, stirring often for 10–12 minutes or until onion just starts to brown. Stir in ¼ cup (50 mL) toasted coarsely chopped almonds, 1 tbsp (15 mL) each brown sugar, balsamic vinegar and chopped fresh sage; heat through. Season with salt and pepper to taste.

Nutrition Per Serving
98 Calories, 5 g Fat, 7 g Protein, 1 g Carbohydrates.
A good source of Iron (20% RDI) and an
excellent source of Zinc (52% RDI)

Orange Ginger Beef Stir-Fry

Delicious and ready in a flash with ready-to-use stir-fry vegetables.

Servings: 4–6
Preparation: 10 minutes
Cooking: 10 minutes

1	1	orange
½ cup	125 mL	Hoisin sauce
1 tbsp	15 mL	each: cornstarch and minced ginger root
½ tsp	2 mL	Chinese 5 spices
¼ tsp	1 mL	dried chili pepper flakes
1 lb	500 g	beef top sirloin grilling steak, ¾-inch (2 cm) thick
2 tsp	10 mL	vegetable oil
2	2	garlic cloves, minced
4 cups	1 L	pre-cut stir-fry vegetables

Finely grate orange peel and squeeze orange juice. Whisk together Hoisin sauce, orange juice, cornstarch, ginger root, Chinese Five Spices, ¼ tsp (1 mL) of the orange peel and pepper flakes; set aside. Cut steak in half lengthwise. Cut crosswise into ¼-inch (5 mm) strips and trim all fat. Heat oil in large non-stick skillet until sizzling hot; stir-fry beef strips and garlic for 2–3 minutes or until beef is browned but still pink inside (cook in 2 batches). Remove beef. Add vegetables and a few spoonfuls of water to skillet; cover and cook 3–4 minutes until tender-crisp. Add reserved sauce and cook, stirring for 2 minutes or until sauce bubbles and thickens. Stir in beef and any juices; heat through. Serve over rice.

TIP: Look for Chinese 5 spices and Hoisin sauce in the Asian sections at your grocery store or at Asian markets.

Nutrition Per Serving
290 Calories, 8 g Fat, 27 g Protein, 27 g Carbohydrates.
An excellent source of Iron (27% RDI) and Zinc (56% RDI)

Original Swiss Steak

Blade steak with the great taste of steak sauce creates this succulent beef dish.

Servings: 4–6
Preparation: 15 minutes
Cooking: 60–90 minutes

1½ lbs	750 g	simmering steak (blade or cross rib)
1	1	bottle (172 mL) steak sauce
½ cup	125 mL	each: red wine (optional) and tomato juice
1	1	medium Spanish onion, cut into strips
1	1	each: small red and green pepper, cut into strips
1 lb	500 g	whole baby new potatoes or regular red potatoes, cut into 2-inch (5 cm) chunks

Season steak with salt and freshly ground pepper to taste. Heat a large lightly-oiled pot over medium-high heat. Brown steak on all sides. Add remaining ingredients, stir well and bring to the boil. Cover and simmer for 60–90 minutes, or until beef is tender. Serve with extra steak sauce.

TIP: If desired, omit red wine and use extra ½ cup (125 mL) tomato juice instead.

Nutrition Per Serving

565 Calories, 10 g Fat, 40 g Protein, 79 g Carbohydrates

Peppered Steaks with Caramelized Onions & Fruit Salsa

The fruit salsa cools down the spiciness. Caramelizing brings out a sweetness.

Servings: 4
Preparation: 15 minutes
Cooking: 28–32 minutes

2	2	red onions
1 tbsp	15 mL	each: olive oil, brown sugar and balsamic vinegar
		Salt and cracked (very coarsely ground) black pepper to taste
½ cup	125 mL	grape tomatoes, halved (or 2 plum tomatoes, diced)
1	1	ripe mango, peeled and diced
⅓ cup	75 mL	diced English cucumber
2 tbsp	30 mL	chopped fresh cilantro
½	½	lime (grated peel, juice and pulp)
4	4	grilling steaks (rib eye, top sirloin, strip loin or tenderloin), 1-inch (2.5 cm) thick

Dice enough red onion to measure ¼ cup (50 mL); reserve for salsa. Cut remaining onions in half and brush with olive oil. Place on grill over medium heat, turning occasionally, for 20 minutes or until fork tender. Transfer onions to medium bowl. With kitchen shears, cut onions into large chunks; stir in brown sugar, balsamic vinegar, salt and pepper to taste. Keep warm until serving time. To prepare salsa combine reserved diced red onion, tomato, mango, cucumber, cilantro, lime peel, juice and pulp in medium bowl; season with salt and pepper to taste and refrigerate. (Salsa may be made several hours in advance.) Meanwhile, season steaks with salt and cracked black pepper (1 tsp/5 mL pepper for a medium-spiced steak). Place steaks on greased grill over medium-high heat; close lid and cook, turning once, for approximately 4–6 minutes per side for rare doneness. Serve each steak with Caramelized Onions and Fruit Salsa, along with focaccia, baguette or any crusty bread.

Nutrition Per Serving
384 Calories, 13 g Fat, 35 g Protein, 34 g Carbohydrates.
A good source of Iron (24% RDI) and an
excellent source of Zinc (79% RDI)

Pizza with Pastrami-Spiced Beef

Once you've tasted this easy gourmet pizza, you may never order take-out again!

Servings: 8
Preparation: 10 minutes
Cooking: 30 minutes
Marinating: 1 hour

1 tbsp	15 mL	each: freshly ground pepper and minced garlic
1½ tsp	7 mL	ground cinnamon
1 tsp	5 mL	each: allspice and salt
¼ tsp	1 mL	cayenne pepper
1 lb	500 g	grilling steak (strip loin or bottom sirloin tri-tip)
2	2	red peppers, cut in quarters
2	2	medium red onions, cut in half
		Olive oil, salt and pepper to taste
½ cup	125 mL	bottled pesto or pizza sauce
4	4	small pizza shells or flatbreads (5–6 inches/12–15 cm)
3 oz	85 g	goat cheese (chèvre)
4 oz	115 g	Havarti cheese, grated

Pastrami spices: combine pepper, garlic, cinnamon, salt, allspice and cayenne pepper in resealable freezer bag. Add beef to spice mixture; seal bag and shake to coat. Refrigerate for 1 hour. Meanwhile, toss peppers and onions with olive oil, salt and pepper; grill over medium heat until tender (about 10 minutes for peppers, 20 minutes for onions). Remove vegetables from grill and cool slightly; cut into equal-sized strips. Spread pesto or pizza sauce evenly over pizza shells or flatbread and top with the peppers, onions and cheeses; set aside. Place steak on greased grill over medium-high heat; close lid and cook, turning once, for approximately 3–4 minutes per side until medium rare (145°F/62°C internally). Remove beef from heat and let sit for 5–10 minutes before slicing thinly. Meanwhile, place pizzas on grill over low heat and cook just until shells are golden brown and cheese is melted. Remove from grill, top pizzas with the sliced steak and serve with side salad.

Nutrition Per Serving
374 Calories, 19 g Fat, 22 g Protein, 28 g Carbohydrates.
A good source of Iron (22% RDI) and an
excellent source of Zinc (29% RDI)

Port Glazed Steak with Poached Pears & Blue Cheese

A truly decadent meal for two!

Servings: 2
Preparation: 5 minutes
Cooking: 20 minutes

1 tbsp	15 mL	butter
1	1	large clove garlic, crushed
½ cup	125 mL	port
¾ cup	175 mL	canned condensed beef broth
1 tbsp	15 mL	dried cranberries
1	1	medium pear, firm but ripe, peeled, cored and sliced in half
2	2	grilling steak (top sirloin, strip loin, tenderloin or rib eye) ½-inch/5 cm thick
½ tsp	2 mL	coarsely ground pepper
2 tbsp	25 mL	crumbled blue cheese (Stilton, Roquefort or Gorgonzola)

In medium skillet melt butter over medium heat; sauté garlic 2–3 minutes, add port and beef broth; bring to boil. Reduce heat to medium, add pear halves and cranberries. Cover and cook just until tender, turning and basting occasionally, about 10–15 minutes. Remove pear halves, cover and set aside. Continue to cook sauce uncovered about 3–4 minutes to reduce sauce to approximately ⅓ cup (75 mL). Meanwhile sprinkle both sides of steaks with pepper. Heat lightly oiled non-stick skillet on medium-high heat; cook steaks about 5–7 minutes for medium-rare. Remove steaks to warm plate and cover; add port sauce to hot skillet to deglaze pan; boil over medium-high for 2–3 minutes or until syrupy. Spoon some sauce onto serving plate; top with steak and half pear. Drizzle remaining sauce over all. Sprinkle crumbled cheese on top of steak. *Serving suggestion*: Serve with rosemary mashed potatoes, squash and broccoli.

Nutrition Per Serving
492 Calories, 21 g Fat, 40 g Protein, 19 g Carbohydrates.
An excellent source of Iron (39% RDI) and Zinc (72% RDI)

Prairie-Style Tri-Tip Steaks

Flavourful yet economical marinating steak in a rye-based marinade.

Servings: 4
Preparation: 5 minutes
Cooking: 10 minutes
Marinating: 8 hours

¼ cup	50 mL	rye whiskey, brandy or apple juice
2 tbsp	30 mL	each: soy sauce and vegetable oil
2	2	cloves garlic, minced
2 tsp	10 mL	brown sugar
1 tsp	5 mL	each: chili powder, dried thyme & coarsely crushed black peppercorns
1½ lb	750 g	marinating steak (flank, round, sirloin tip or tri-tip) ¾-inch (2 cm) thick (approx 4 steaks)

In resealable freezer bag, combine whiskey, soy sauce, oil, garlic, sugar, chili powder, thyme and peppercorns. Add steaks to bag; seal tightly and refrigerate 8–24 hours for maximum flavour. Discard marinade. Grill, broil or sauté using medium-high heat for 4–5 minutes per side for medium doneness — best cooked only to medium. Serve with grilled vegetables and mashed potatoes.

Nutrition Per Serving
281 Calories, 13 g Fat, 37 g Protein, 1 g Carbohydrates.
A good source of Iron (24% RDI) and an
excellent source of Zinc (102% RDI)

Raclette-Style Beef in Herbed Butter

If you don't own a raclette, you can always sauté in a non-stick pan.

Servings: 4
Preparation: 10 minutes
Cooking: 10 minutes

2	2	garlic cloves
¼ tsp	1 mL	salt
½ cup	125 mL	softened unsalted butter
¼ cup	50 mL	chopped fresh Italian parsley
1 tbsp	15 mL	chopped fresh rosemary and/or sage
2 tbsp	30 mL	lemon juice
2 tsp	10 mL	Dijon mustard
		Freshly ground pepper
1 lb	500 g	grilling steak (tenderloin, strip loin, top sirloin or rib eye), cut into ¼-inch (0.5 cm) thick strips

Coarsely chop garlic cloves. Using the side of a chef's knife (at the tip), rub the garlic and salt together using circular motions until paste-like. Combine with remaining ingredients (except beef). (Note: Herbed Butter can be made ahead and frozen. Use any extra Herbed Butter for later meals, stirring into mashed potatoes or steamed vegetables.) Heat raclette until sizzling hot, placing pots of cheese under the grill to melt. Sauté the beef strips and vegetables on the raclette in melted herbed butter until browned. Dip beef and vegetables into melted cheeses and serve with mayonnaise and pickles.

TIP: Use melted Camembert or other soft cheese and Dijon-flavoured mayonnaise as dips.

Nutrition Per Serving

297 Calories, 21 g Fat, 26 g Protein, 1 g Carbohydrates

Ranch-style Beef Kabobs & Rice

Use ranch salad dressing as a brushing sauce for beef and vegetables.

Servings: 4
Cooking: 30 minutes
Marinating: ½–1 hour

1 lb	500 g	marinating steak (round or sirloin tip) or grilling steak (sirloin, strip loin, rib eye or tenderloin), cut 1-inch (2.5 cm) thick
1	1	package (165 g) packaged beef flavoured rice
1	1	each: green, yellow and red bell peppers, cut into 1-inch (2.5 cm) pieces
1	1	package (28 g) ranch creamy salad dressing mix
1 tbsp	15 mL	vegetable oil

Trim fat, if any, from beef steak. Cut steak into 1–1¼ inch (2.5–3 cm) pieces. Marinate beef cubes in ranch dressing for 30 minutes to 1 hour before grilling. Prepare rice according to package directions. Alternately thread equal amounts of beef and vegetables onto each of four 12-inch (30 cm) metal skewers. In small bowl, combine dressing mix, 2 tbsp (30 mL) water and oil; mix well. If dressing is too thick add more water. Brush onto all sides of kabobs. Barbecue or broil on rack approximately 8–11 minutes until beef is medium-rare to medium doneness and vegetables are crisp-tender, turning occasionally. Brush kabobs with any remaining dressing mixture during first 5 minutes of grilling. Serve on bed of rice.

Nutrition Per Serving

335 Calories, 8.6 g Fat, 29 g Protein, 35 g Carbohydrates

Spanish Fiesta Steak

Olé! This quick and colourful recipe is long on flavour, short on time and effort.

Servings: 4
Preparation: 5 minutes
Cooking: 15 minutes

1 lb	500 g	4 grilling steaks (top sirloin or strip loin), ¾-inch (2 cm) thick
1	1	each: red and green pepper, cut into narrow strips
1	1	can (12 oz/341 mL) whole kernel corn
1	1	can (10 oz/284 mL) tomato soup
1 tbsp	15 mL	lemon juice
½ tsp	2 mL	cumin or 1 tsp (5 mL) chili powder — optional

Heat a large oiled skillet over medium-high heat; brown steaks 3–4 minutes on each side. Place steaks on a plate and cover loosely. Reduce heat under skillet and add peppers; stir and cook 3–4 minutes or until softened. Add corn with liquid, tomato soup, lemon juice, any juices accumulated on steak plate and cumin or chili powder, if using. Cook 3–5 minutes. Slice steak and serve with vegetable medley and corn chips, or in soft tortillas.

Nutrition Per Serving

254 Calories, 7 g Fat, 23 g Protein, 25 g Carbohydrates

Steak and Smoked Salmon Roll

Here's a wonderful and not-so-common combination of smoked salmon and beef.

Servings: 4–6
Preparation: 15–20 minutes
Cooking: 30–40 minutes

1½ lb	750 g	marinating steak (flank, tip or round), ¾-inch (2 cm) thick
4 oz	125 g	light spreadable cream cheese
4 oz	125 g	thinly sliced smoked salmon
2	2	green onions, finely chopped
		Pepper to taste

If possible, have butcher pass the steak through a mechanical tenderizing machine. With a mallet, pound steak to about ½-inch (1 cm) thickness. Spread with cream cheese to within ¼ inch (0.5 cm) of edge. Sprinkle with green onions and pepper. Cover completely with smoked salmon slices. Starting with long side, roll up like a jelly roll. Tie tightly in several places with butcher's twine, or hold together with metal skewers. Barbecue over medium-high heat 400°F (200°C) for 30–40 minutes, turning approximately every 8 minutes to brown all sides. Insert a meat thermometer into the centre of the roll and cook until it reads at least 155°F (68°C). Remove roll from grill; place seam-side-down on cutting board and tent with foil for 5 minutes. Remove string and cut into slices. Serve with salad greens or steamed broccoli and new potatoes.

Nutrition Per Serving

258 Calories, 13 g Fat, 31 g Protein, 1.7 g Carbohydrates

Steak Diane

Back by popular demand—this classic has been updated for the new century.

Servings: 4
Cooking: 25 minutes

1	1	pkg (approx 34 g) brown gravy mix
2 tbsp	30 mL	butter
1	1	lemon, cut into 6 wedges
1 lb	500 g	4 grilling steaks (strip loin, rib eye, top sirloin or tenderloin)
2	2	shallots or green onions, chopped
1 tbsp	15 mL	each: chopped fresh parsley and tomato paste
¼ tsp	1 mL	Worcestershire sauce
1 tbsp	15 mL	sherry
¼ cup	50 mL	cognac or brandy
		Salt and pepper to taste

Prepare gravy mix according to package directions; set aside. In skillet melt butter over medium heat. Using a fork, rub 3 lemon wedges around sides and bottom of pan, squeezing juice into butter. Discard any lemon seeds. Add steak to pan and sear both sides. Stir in shallots, parsley, tomato paste, Worcestershire sauce and prepared gravy. Bring to low boil; simmer for 3–5 minutes or until steak is cooked to desired doneness. Add sherry. In 1 cup (250 mL) microwavable glass measure, microwave cognac on high for 30 seconds or until warm. Carefully ignite with match. While flaming, pour over steak (or add to sauce). Serve steak immediately with sauce. Garnish with remaining lemon wedges and season to taste.

Nutrition Per Serving

289 Calories, 15 g Fat, 25 g Protein, 6.3 g Carbohydrates.
A good source of Iron (24% RDI) and an
excellent source of Zinc (46% RDI)

Strip Loins in Wine Sauce

Another easy sauce idea for beef strip loins.

Servings: 4
Cooking: 20 minutes

4	4	grilling steaks (strip loin, top sirloin, tenderloin or rib eye), cut 1-inch thick
1 tbsp	15 mL	melted butter
1 tbsp	15 mL	dry red wine
2 tbsp	30 mL	chopped green onions
2 cups	500 mL	sliced mushrooms
½ cup	125 mL	dry red wine
1 cup	250 mL	beef stock
		pinch of dried thyme

Brush steaks with mixture of 1 tbsp (15 mL) each melted butter and dry red wine. Season with pepper. Broil using medium high heat for 5–7 minutes per side for rare or 7–9 minutes per side for medium, turning once with tongs. While steaks broil, sauté green onions and mushrooms in oiled non-stick pan until softened. Add dry red wine, beef stock and thyme.

Nutrition Per Serving

364 Calories, 16 g Fat, 45 g Protein, 2.7 g Carbohydrates

T-Bone Steaks with Pistou

A quick meal made with steaks taken directly from the freezer.

Servings: 4
Preparation: 10 minutes
Cooking: 10–15 minutes

2	2	cloves garlic, finely chopped
⅓ cup	75 mL	fresh basil (or 1½ tsp/7 mL dried)
⅓ cup	75 mL	freshly grated Parmesan cheese
1 tbsp	15 mL	tomato paste
1 tbsp	15 mL	olive oil
4	4	T-bone grilling steaks (½-inch/1 cm thick)
1	1	bag (2 lb/1 kg) baby potatoes

In a bowl, pound garlic and basil into a paste. Mix in Parmesan cheese and tomato paste; beat in olive oil. Broil steaks on one side for 4–5 minutes for rare, or 5–7 minutes for medium; turn steak and broil for an additional 2–3 minutes for rare or 3–4 minutes for medium. Remove steaks and spread each steak with ¼ Pistou mixture, return to broiler for an additional 2–3 minutes (allowing slightly less time for fresh/defrosted steaks). Meanwhile, boil baby potatoes. Serve steaks with baby potatoes and steamed vegetables.

Nutrition Per Serving

550 Calories, 21 g Fat, 49 g Protein, 39 g Carbohydrates

Thai Beef Stir-Fry

Experience a delicious taste of the Far East with this quick and easy stir-fry.

Servings: 4
Preparation: 5 minutes
Cooking: 10 minutes

2	2	packages (each 3 oz/85 g) instant soup noodles, beef flavour
1 lb	500 g	beef stir-fry strips or marinating steak (i.e., inside round or sirloin tip), cut into strips
2 tsp	10 mL	minced garlic or 1 tsp (5 mL) garlic powder
4 tsp	20 mL	minced ginger root
½	½	package (750 g) frozen Oriental vegetables or 1½ cups (375 mL) fresh snowpeas & red pepper strips
⅔ cup	150 mL	orange juice
2 tbsp	30 mL	bottled stir-fry sauce (i.e., Thai, Szechwan)

Place noodles in shallow casserole; sprinkle with 1 packet seasoning mix, cover with boiling water and set aside. Heat garlic and ginger root in a large oiled skillet over medium-high heat. Sprinkle beef with contents of remaining seasoning packet and place in skillet, stir-fry just until beef loses its pink colour. Remove meat from pan. Add vegetables and stir-fry 2 minutes. Add drained noodles and cook one minute more. Stir in orange juice, stir-fry sauce and meat. Cook and stir until well blended. Serve immediately.

Nutrition Per Serving

423 Calories, 11 g Fat, 37 g Protein, 45 g Carbohydrates

Two Tomato Beef Pasta

This Mediterranean style beef pasta dish is easy to prepare and ready in minutes.

Servings: 4
Preparation: 10 minutes
Cooking: 10 minutes

6	6	sun-dried tomatoes
1 lb	500 g	beef stir-fry strips or top sirloin grilling steak, cut into strips
3	3	cloves garlic, minced
½	½	small red onion, sliced
1	1	medium zucchini, sliced
4	4	fresh plum tomatoes, chopped
½ cup	125 mL	chopped fresh basil
12 oz	375 g	penne pasta, cooked and drained
		freshly grated Parmesan cheese (optional)

In bowl, cover dried tomatoes with boiling water; let stand 5 minutes. Drain and chop into strips. In large lightly oiled non-stick skillet, stir-fry beef and garlic over high heat, until beef is no longer pink. Remove meat from pan. In same skillet, cook sun-dried tomatoes, onion and zucchini over medium-high heat until softened, about 2 minutes. Add chopped tomatoes and stir-fry 2 minutes longer. Return beef (with juices) to skillet with basil, salt and pepper to taste; mix well and heat through briefly. Toss with hot cooked pasta. Serve immediately with Parmesan cheese, if desired.

TIP: Replace fresh basil with 1½ tsp (7 mL) dried, but add to skillet with chopped tomatoes.

Nutrition Per Serving
387 Calories, 5 g Fat, 27 g Protein, 58 g Carbohydrates.
An excellent source of Iron (38% RDI) and Zinc (43% RDI)

Weeknight Steak Dinner

There is nothing quite like a meal of barbecued steak with Caesar salad and potatoes.

Servings: 4–6
Preparation: 5 minutes
Cooking: 12 minutes
Marinating: 8–12 hours

¾ cup	175 mL	soy sauce
¼ cup	50 mL	packed brown sugar
1	1	garlic clove, minced
1 tbsp	15 mL	minced fresh ginger root
1½ lb	750 g	marinating steaks (inside round, sirloin tip, outside round or flank), or grilling steaks (rib eye, top sirloin, tenderloin or strip loin), 1-inch (2.5 cm) thick

Combine all ingredients (except beef) in large sealable freezer bag. Pierce steak all over with fork; add to bag and refrigerate for 8–12 hours. Discard marinade. Grill or broil steak using medium-high heat for 6–7 minutes/side for medium. After grilling slice steak thinly across the grain to serve.

Garlic Smashed Potatoes: Boil scrubbed 3-inch (7.5 cm) new potatoes until just tender. Drain and cool slightly. Flatten each potato slightly with your hand, keeping potatoes intact. Brush generously with your favourite salad dressing and season with some minced garlic, salt and pepper. Grill about 3 minutes/side, until crispy and browned.

TIP: Grilling steaks are marinated briefly — 15 minutes or up to 1 hour — just for flavour.

Nutrition Per Serving

200 Calories, 11 g Fat, 24 g Protein, 1 g Carbohydrates

Beef & Portobello Stew

Serve this versatile stew in edible bowls made of hollowed-out large crusty rolls.

Servings: 4–6
Preparation: 20 minutes
Cooking: 1½ hours

⅓ cup	75 mL	all-purpose flour
½ tsp	2 mL	each: salt and dried thyme
¼ tsp	1 mL	each: pepper and crushed dried rosemary
1 lb	500 g	stewing beef cubes
2 tbsp	30 mL	vegetable oil or butter
½ cup	125 mL	leeks (white part only), shallots or onions, chopped
1	1	clove garlic, minced
4 cups	1 L	coarsely chopped portobello mushrooms (1-inch/2.5 cm chunks)
2½ cups	625 mL	beef broth or stock
½ cup	125 mL	dry red wine
1 tbsp	15 mL	tomato paste
		salt and pepper to taste

In shallow bowl, combine flour, salt, thyme, pepper and rosemary. Coat beef cubes lightly with flour mixture, reserving any remaining flour mixture to thicken stew. In Dutch oven or stockpot, heat oil over medium heat. Brown beef cubes on all sides in batches. Add leeks, garlic and mushrooms to browned beef; cook until leeks are soft, about 5 minutes. Gradually stir in broth, scraping up brown bits from bottom of pan. Stir in wine and tomato paste; mix well. Bring to boil; reduce heat, cover and simmer for 1½ hours or until meat is tender. To thicken, whisk 2–3 tablespoons (30–45 mL) cold water into reserved flour mixture until smooth. Gradually whisk into bubbling stew. Cook and stir until sauce thickens. Season with salt and pepper.

Nutrition Per Serving
128 Calories, 7 g Fat, 19 g Protein, 9 g Carbohydrates.
A good source of Iron (20% RDI) and an
excellent source of Zinc (50% RDI)

Beef Bourguignon

A traditional favourite for turning an inexpensive cut of beef into an elegant meal.

Servings: 6
Preparation: 25 minutes
Cooking: 2½ hours

4	4	slices bacon, diced
2	2	medium onions, cut lengthwise into slices
8 oz	250 g	mushrooms, halved
2 lb	1 kg	stewing beef cubes
3 tbsp	45 mL	all-purpose flour
3	3	garlic cloves, minced
1½ cups	375 mL	each: red wine and beef broth
1	1	bay leaf
1 tsp	5 mL	dried thyme
½ tsp	2 mL	each: salt and pepper

Pan-fry bacon in Dutch oven or heavy stockpot using medium-high heat until lightly browned. Remove bacon; set aside. Sauté onion and mushrooms in bacon fat until just browned. Remove vegetables; set aside. Brown beef in two batches, adding some vegetable oil, if necessary. Sprinkle flour over browned meat. Add garlic, wine, broth, bay leaf, thyme, salt and pepper. Cook, covered, in 325°F (160°C) oven for 2 hours. Add reserved bacon, onion and mushrooms; cook 30 minutes longer.

Nutrition Per Serving

381 Calories, 19 g Fat, 41 g Protein, 9 g Carbohydrates

Chunky Beef Chili

Cook large batches and freeze in family-sized portions.

Servings: 8–10
Preparation: 10–15 minutes
Cooking: 30–45 minutes
Marinating: 30 minutes

1	1	pouch quick stew mix
2 lbs	1 kg	stewing beef cubes
2	2	onions, chopped
2	2	green peppers, chopped
4	4	cans 14 oz/398 mL chili-style stewed tomatoes
2	2	cans 14 oz/398 mL kidney beans (do NOT drain)
1½ cups	375 mL	rice
2 tbsp	30 mL	cocoa powder

Mix quick stew pouch with water according to package directions. Marinate beef for 30 minutes in large pot. Bring meat mixture to a boil and stir in remaining ingredients plus 2 cups (500 mL) water. Cover and simmer for at least 30 minutes. Serve with tortillas, taco chips or crusty rolls and a salad.

TIP: You can omit the quick stew mix and brown the beef cubes in a large, lightly oiled pot. Add 3 cups (750 mL) water and remaining ingredients and cook for at least 1½ hours.

Time Saver: You can make this chili in 20–30 minutes by substituting ground beef or cubed, cooked beef and omitting the quick stew mix.

Nutrition Per Serving

489 Calories, 9.1 g Fat, 35 g Protein, 68 g Carbohydrates

Country Beef Ragout

This delicious stew can also be made in the slow cooker on high for 5–6 hours.

Servings: 4
Preparation: 15 minutes
Cooking: 2½ hours

1 lb	500 g	stewing beef cubes
1	1	large onion, cut in wedges
1	1	clove garlic, crushed
2	2	large celery stalks, cut in 1-inch (2.5 cm) pieces
1	1	can (28 oz/796 mL) whole seasoned tomatoes
½ tsp	2 mL	dried thyme
½ cup	125 mL	dry red wine
1 tsp	5 mL	concentrated liquid beef stock
1 cup	250 mL	mushrooms, quartered

Brown beef cubes on all sides in a large lightly oiled skillet. Remove and place in an oven-proof casserole. In the skillet, cook onions, garlic and celery for 2–3 minutes and stir in remaining ingredients, except mushrooms. Bring to boil, stirring constantly. Season with salt and pepper and pour over beef. Cover casserole and place in preheated 350°F (180°C) oven. After 1 hour, add mushrooms and cook for another 1½ hours, removing lid for last 15 minutes. Serve over noodles or garlic mashed potatoes.

TIP: To make this stew in a hurry, mix 1 pouch (approx 56 g) quick stew mix with water according to package directions. Add beef and marinate in pot for 30 minutes. Bring to a boil, add remaining ingredients (using a 14 oz/398 mL can of tomatoes instead) and simmer covered for 20–30 minutes.

Nutrition Per Serving

249 Calories, 8.7 g Fat, 29 g Protein, 14 g Carbohydrates

Curried Beef Stew

Warm up your taste buds with the exotic taste of this simple stew.

Servings: 4
Preparation: 5–10 minutes
Cooking: 2 hours

⅓ cup	75 mL	chopped onion
2 tbsp	30 mL	curry powder
1	1	bay leaf
1 lb	500 g	stewing beef cubes
½ cup	125 mL	each: shredded cabbage and carrots (or 1 cup/250 mL bagged coleslaw mix)
½ cup	125 mL	chopped green onion

In large, lightly oiled frypan, combine first 3 ingredients and 1 cup (250 mL) water. Cook over medium heat for 2 minutes. Add beef and simmer covered on stove or in 325°F (160°C) oven for 1¾ hours. Add vegetables and cook covered for another 15 minutes. Season with salt and pepper to taste. Remove bay leaf and serve with rice.

TIP: To make this stew in a hurry, mix 1 pouch (approx 56 g) quick stew mix with water according to package directions. Add beef and marinate in pot for 30 minutes. Bring to a boil, add first 3 ingredients and simmer covered for 15 minutes. Add cabbage, carrots and green onion and cook covered for another 15 minutes.

Nutrition Per Serving

284 Calories, 11 g Fat, 29 g Protein, 5.6 g Carbohydrates

Homestyle Beef Stew

New stew mixes tenderize quickly using natural ingredients found in fruit.

Servings: 6
Preparation: 30 minutes
Cooking: 20–30 minutes

1	1	package quick stew mix
1 lb	500 g	beef stewing cubes, blade or cross rib simmering steak or boneless simmering short ribs, cut in 1½-inch (3.5 cm) cubes
8 cups	2 L	fresh, frozen or canned vegetables, cut in chunks (i.e., carrots, onions, potatoes, celery, tomatoes, mushrooms, peas and/or green beans)
1 tsp	5 mL	dried thyme leaves
1	1	can (10 oz/284 mL) beef broth
½ cup	125 mL	burgundy cooking wine (optional)

Mix stew marinade pouch with water according to package directions and marinate meat in large covered pot for 30 minutes. Bring meat and liquid to a boil. Season to taste with pepper. Add remaining ingredients and stir. Cover, reduce heat and simmer for 20–30 minutes. Thicken with a mixture of 2 tbsp (30 mL) each of flour and water, if desired. Serve over noodles or with toast.

TIP: You can omit quick stew mix and brown beef cubes over medium high heat in a lightly oiled pot. Add an extra 1 cup (250 mL) water and remaining ingredients (except vegetables) and cook covered for 2 hours on stove top or in 325°F (160°C) oven. Add vegetables for the last half hour.

Nutrition Per Serving

234 Calories, 6 g Fat, 21 g Protein, 24 g Carbohydrates

Maple-Glazed Beef

A hint of maple adds character to this comfort food.

Servings: 6
Preparation: 10 minutes
Cooking: 1¾ hours

2 lbs	1 kg	stewing cubes or boneless beef simmering short ribs (if bone-in, use 3 lbs/1.5 kg)
2	2	medium onions, sliced
1	1	celery stalk with leaves, sliced
½ cup	125 mL	maple syrup
2 tbsp	30 mL	each: cider vinegar and chili sauce (or mild salsa)
1 tsp	5 mL	each: Worcestershire sauce, dry mustard and bottled gravy browning liquid
3 tbsp	45 mL	quick-cooking tapioca*

Combine all ingredients plus 2 cups (500 mL) water in large pot. Season with salt and pepper to taste. Cover and simmer on stove or in 325°F (160°C) oven for 1¾ hours. Skim off fat and remove bones, if any. Serve with crusty rolls or French bread.

* Omit tapioca and mix ¼ cup (50 mL) cornstarch or flour with ¼ cup (50 mL) water to make a paste. Turn the heat to High 15 minutes before serving and stir in the paste. Cook until it boils and thickens.

TIP: Combine all ingredients plus 1 cup (250 mL) water in 4 quart (4 L) slow cooker. Season with salt and pepper to taste. Cover and cook on High for 4–5 hours (or on low for 8–10 hours).

Nutrition Per Serving

309 Calories, 9.9 g Fat, 21 g Protein, 27 g Carbohydrates

Pastry-Topped Ginger Beef

A great cook-ahead dish for a large buffet and you can freeze the leftovers.

Servings: 4–6
Preparation: 15 minutes
Cooking: 2½–3½ hours

¼ cup	50 mL	cornstarch
2	2	cans (10 oz/284 mL) consomme soup
1	1	envelope (35 g) dried onion roasted garlic soup mix
½ cup	125 mL	cooking sherry
¼ cup	50 mL	grated ginger root (fresh or jarred)
		freshly ground pepper to taste
3 lbs	1.5 kg	beef stewing cubes, or oven roast or marinating steak cut into cubes (round, sirloin tip or flank)
1 lb	500 g	fresh baby carrots
1	1	package (397 g) frozen puff pastry

In a Dutch oven or large pot, mix together first 6 ingredients. Add meat and mix well. Cover and simmer on stovetop or bake in 300°F (150°C) oven for 2–3 hours until beef is fork tender.* Meanwhile, on a lightly floured surface, roll pastry into a large rectangle. Add carrots to beef mixture and transfer to a large rectangular 3 qt (3 L) casserole and cover with pastry. Trim edges, cut steam holes and decorate with extra pieces of pastry. Bake in a 400°F (200°C) oven for 30 minutes or until golden and filling is bubbly.

TIP: *Recipe may be prepared to this stage and then refrigerated and finished the next day.

Nutrition Per Serving

383 Calories, 19 g Fat, 27 g Protein, 22 g Carbohydrates

Simple Beef Goulash

Here's a wonderful option for your slow cooker.

Servings: 8
Preparation: 20–25 minutes
Cooking: 5–6 hours—high/10–12 hours—low

2 lbs	1 kg	beef pot roast (brisket, cross rib or short rib), cut in 1-inch (2.5 cm) cubes or stewing beef cubes
1	1	pouch (38.5 g) onion soup mix
2 tbsp	30 mL	paprika
¼ tsp	1 mL	caraway seeds
¼ cup	50 mL	quick-cooking tapioca*
1	1	can (10 oz/284 mL) whole mushrooms (do NOT drain)
8 cups	2 L	vegetables, cut in small chunks (e.g., carrots, potatoes, rutabaga or turnip, parsnip and/or green pepper)

Place ingredients plus 1½ cups (375 mL) water in a 4 qt (4 L) slow cooker. Stir, cover and cook on high for 5–6 hours (or on low for 10–12 hours). Serve goulash with dumplings or over hot cooked noodles or rice.

* Omit tapioca and mix ¼ cup (50 mL) cornstarch or flour with ¼ cup (50 mL) water to make a paste. Turn the heat to High 15 minutes before serving and stir in the paste. Cook until it boils and thickens.

TIP: If you don't have a slow cooker, brown the beef cubes in a large lightly oiled pot. Add an extra 1½ cups (375 mL) water and remaining ingredients (except vegetables) and cook covered for at least 2 hours on stove top or in a 325°F (160°C) oven. Add vegetables for last half hour of cooking time.

Nutrition Per Serving

280 Calories, 8.8 g Fat, 23 g Protein, 28 g Carbohydrates

Traditional Braised Beef Stew

What could be more satisfying than a big bowl of hearty stew?

Servings: 8
Preparation: 25 minutes
Cooking: 1½ hours

2 tbsp	30 mL	olive or vegetable oil
2 lb	1 kg	stewing beef cubes
¼ cup	50 mL	all-purpose flour
2	2	garlic cloves, minced
1	1	large onion, cut lengthwise into eighths
1 cup	250 mL	beef broth
28 oz	796 mL	can diced plum tomatoes
2 tbsp	30 mL	each: Worcestershire sauce and balsamic vinegar
1 tsp	5 mL	dried thyme (or 4–5 sprigs of fresh thyme)
1	1	bay leaf
½ tsp	2 mL	each: salt and pepper
2	2	carrots, cut into 1-inch (2.5 cm) chunks
½ lb	250 g	scrubbed mini potatoes, quartered
		Chopped fresh parsley

Heat oil in Dutch oven or stockpot over medium-high heat until sizzling hot. Brown meat in 4 batches. Set beef aside; sprinkle with flour. Add garlic and onion to pot, cooking 3–4 minutes until just softened, adding more oil if necessary. Stir in broth, scraping up browned bits from the bottom. Add reserved beef, tomatoes, Worcestershire, vinegar, thyme, salt, pepper and bay leaf. Bring to a simmer. Simmer, covered, on stove-top or in 325°F (160°C) oven for 1 hour until fork tender. Add vegetables and cook 30–40 minutes longer or until vegetables are tender. Garnish each serving with some chopped parsley.

Nutrition Per Serving
289 Calories, 12 g Fat, 28 g Protein, 17 g Carbohydrates.
An excellent source of Iron (26% RDI) and Zinc (74% RDI)

Index

All Kinds O' Meatballs 37
Appetizer
  Layered Cuban Dip 46
  Tangy Thai Beef Pinwheels 32
Asian Hot Pot 88
Asian Rotisserie Roast with Tropical Salsa 65
Autumn Steak with Mulling Spices 89

Balsamic-Beer Flank Steak 90
Barbecue
  Balsamic-Beer Flank Steak 90
  BBQ "Five Spiced" Beef Roast 66
  BBQ Flank Steak "Parisienne" 91
  BBQ Steak with Saucy Mushrooms 92
  Best BBQ Beef Oven Roast 67
  Grilled Beef Tenderloin with Goat Cheese 104
  Involtini of Sirloin Steak 105
  Key Lime BBQ Beef Roast 76
  Key Lime Steaks 107
  Louis' Cola-Kiwi Steaks 109
  Middle Eastern Grilled Steak Pockets 112
  Peppered Steaks with Caramelized Onions & Fruit
    Salsa 117
  Prairie-Style Tri-Tip Steaks 120
  Weeknight Steak Dinner 130
BBQ "Five Spiced" Beef Roast 66
BBQ Flank Steak "Parisienne" 91
BBQ Steak with Saucy Mushrooms 92
Beef & Portobello Stew 131
Beef & Spinach Salad with Cream Cheese & Candied
    Pecans 19
Beef and Barley Soup 18
Beef and Orange Kabobs 93
Beef Bourguignon 132
Beef Moussaka 38
Beef Salad on the Wild Side 20
Beef Tart-ieres 39
Best BBQ Beef Oven Roast 67
Bombay Beef & Cauliflower 94
Bourguignon
  Beef Bourguignon 132
  Quick 'n Easy Beef Bourguignon 60

Brandied Beef Tenderloin 68
Brewed Beef with Roasted Root Vegetables 95
Bruschetta
  Greek Beef Bruschetta 42
Burgers
  International Burgers 44
  M-M-Marvellous Mushroom Burgers 50
  The Prairie Burger 52

Cajun Pot Roast 69
Caribbean Quick Roast 70
Cheese Crowned Tenderloins 96
Chili
  Chunky Beef Chili 133
Chinese Steak Salad 21
Chunky Beef Chili 133
Cinnamon Braised Beef 97
Cooked Beef
  Layered Mediterranean Loaf 26
  Potstickers 29
  Tangy Thai Beef Pinwheels 32
  Thai Beef Wraps 34
Country Beef Ragout 134
Creole Mustard Beef Oscar 98
Curried Beef and Lentils 40
Curried Beef Stew 135

Dijon Beef and Greens 22

Easy Asian Steak 99
Empañadas de Picadillo 41
English Pub-Style Beef 100

Fajitas
  Fantastic Beef Fajitas 101
  Flaming Fajitas 103
Fantastic Beef Fajitas 101
Festive Cranberry Pot Roast 71
Fettucine with Roasted Red Pepper & Garlic Cream
    Sauce 102
Fish
  Steak and Smoked Salmon Roll 124

Flaming Fajitas 103
Fondue
  Asian Hot Pot 88

Ginger Beef
  Ginger Beef Salad 23
  Orange Ginger Beef Stir-Fry 115
  Pastry-Topped Ginger Beef 138
  Sesame Ginger Beef Stir-Fry 61
Ginger Beef Salad 23
Greek Beef Bruschetta 42
Greek Steak Sandwich 55
Grilled Beef Tenderloin with Goat Cheese 104
Ground Beef
  All Kinds O' Meatballs 37
  Beef Moussaka 38
  Beef Tart-ieres 39
  Curried Beef and Lentils 40
  Empañadas de Picadillo 41
  Greek Beef Bruschetta 42
  Hearty Beef Pizza 43
  International Burgers 44
  Korean Beef with Lettuce Cups 45
  Layered Cuban Dip 46
  M-M-Marvellous Mushroom Burgers 50
  Make-Ahead Mexican Lasagna 47
  Meatballs with Roasted Vegetables and Garlic 48
  Mexican Hot Pot 49
  Muffin-Sized Pizza Meat Loaves 51
  Prairie Burger 52
  Simple Meat Sauce 53
  Spiced Beef Stuffed Peppers 54

Harvest Beef Kabobs 56
Hawaiian Beef Stir-Fry 57
Hearty Beef Pizza 43
Herb & Mustard "Plastered" Rotisserie Roast 72
Herb Medley Beef Roast 73
Holiday Roast with Portobello Sauce 74
Homestyle Beef Stew 136

International Burgers 44
Involtini of Sirloin Steak 105
Italian Beef Soup 24
Italian Herb Roast 75

Japanese Steak Salad 25
Java Pepper Steak 106

Kabobs
  Beef and Orange Kabobs 93
  Harvest Beef Kabobs 56
  Ranch-Style Beef Kabobs & Rice 122
Key Lime BBQ Beef Roast 76
Key Lime Steaks 107
Korean Beef with Lettuce Cups 45

Lasagna
  Make-Ahead Mexican Lasagna 47
Layered Cuban Dip 46
Layered Mediterranean Loaf 26
Lemon Pepper Steak For Two 108
Louis' Cola-Kiwi Steaks 109
Low-Fat Honey Dijon Marinated Steak 110

M-M-Marvellous Mushroom Burgers 50
Make-Ahead Mexican Lasagna 47
Mandarin Orange Pepper Steak 111
Maple-Glazed Beef 137
Meatballs with Roasted Vegetables and Garlic 48
Mediterranean Beef Stir-Fry 58
Mediterranean Pasta Salad with BBQ Roast Beef 27
Mexican Hot Pot 49
Middle Eastern Grilled Steak Pockets 112
Moroccan Beef with Tabbouleh 113
Moroccan Spiced Quick Roast with Kasbah
      Couscous 77
Muffin-Sized Pizza Meat Loaves 51
Mustard Medallions with Sage Onion Compote 114

Orange Ginger Beef Stir-Fry 115
Original Swiss Steak 116

Pacific Rim Rotisserie Roast 78
Pasta
  Fettucine with Roasted Red Pepper & Garlic Cream
      Sauce 102
  Mediterranean Pasta Salad with BBQ Roast Beef 27
  Two Tomato Beef Pasta 129
Pastry-Topped Ginger Beef 138
Peppered Steaks with Caramelized Onions & Fruit
      Salsa 117

Pizza-Style Minute Steaks 59
Pizza with Pastrami-Spiced Beef 118
Pomegranate & Citrus Beef Salad 28
Port Glazed Steak with Poached Pears & Blue Cheese
    119
Potstickers 29
Prairie Burger 52
Prairie-Style Tri-Tip Steaks 120

Quick 'n Easy Beef Bourguignon 60
Quick Serve
  Greek Steak Sandwich 55
  Harvest Beef Kabobs 56
  Hawaiian Beef Stir-Fry 57
  Mediterranean Beef Stir-Fry 58
  Pizza-Style Minute Steaks 59
  Quick 'n Easy Beef Bourguignon 60
  Sesame Ginger Beef Stir-Fry 61
  Steak and Pepper Heroes 62
  Thai Beef Satay 63
  Thai Spicy Beef with Noodles 64

Raclette-Style Beef in Herbed Butter 121
Ranch-Style Beef Kabobs & Rice 122
Ribs
  Tex-Mex Ribs 87
Roasts
  Asian Rotisserie Roast with Tropical Salsa 65
  BBQ "Five Spiced" Beef Roast 66
  Best BBQ Beef Oven Roast 67
  Brandied Beef Tenderloin 68
  Cajun Pot Roast 69
  Caribbean Quick Roast 70
  Festive Cranberry Pot Roast 71
  Herb & Mustard "Plastered" Rotisserie Roast 72
  Herb Medley Beef Roast 73
  Holiday Roast with Portobello Sauce 74
  Italian Herb Roast 75
  Key Lime BBQ Beef Roast 76
  Moroccan Spiced Quick Roast with Kasbah
    Couscous 77
  Pacific Rim Rotisserie Roast 78
  Roast Beef with Harvest Vegetables 79
  Rosemary Pot Roast with Braised Vegetables 80
  Ruby-Glazed Roast Beef 81
  Rush-Hour Roast Beef Dinner 82

  Savoury Sunday Roast 83
  Stuffed Cranberry Roast 84
  Surf & Turf Beef Roast 85
  Tangy Oktoberfest Roast 86
  Tex-Mex Ribs 87
Roast Beef with Harvest Vegetables 79
Rosemary Pot Roast with Braised Vegetables 80
Ruby-Glazed Roast Beef 81
Rush-Hour Roast Beef Dinner 82

Salads
  Beef & Spinach with Cream Cheese & Candied
    Pecans 19
  Beef Salad on the Wild Side 20
  Chinese Steak Salad 21
  Dijon Beef and Greens 22
  Ginger Beef Salad 23
  Japanese Steak Salad 25
  Mediterranean Pasta Salad with BBQ Roast Beef 27
  Pomegranate & Citrus Beef Salad 28
  Spicy Beef & Rice Salad 30
  Spinach Salad with Steak and Strawberries 31
  Teriyaki Surf & Turf Salad 33
  Warm Beef & Berry Salad 36
Savoury Sunday Roast 83
Sesame Ginger Beef Stir-Fry 61
Simple Beef Goulash 139
Simple Meat Sauce 53
Soups
  Beef and Barley 18
  Italian Beef Soup 24
  Vietnamese Soup 35
Spanish Fiesta Steak 123
Spiced Beef Stuffed Peppers 54
Spicy Beef & Rice Salad 30
Spinach Salad with Steak and Strawberries 31
Steak
  Asian Hot Pot 88
  Autumn Steak with Mulling Spices 89
  Balsamic-Beer Flank Steak 90
  BBQ Flank Steak "Parisienne" 91
  BBQ Steak with Saucy Mushrooms 92
  Beef and Orange Kabobs 93
  Bombay Beef & Cauliflower 94
  Brandied Beef Tenderloin 68
  Brewed Beef with Roasted Root Vegetables 95

Cheese Crowned Tenderloins 96
Cinnamon Braised Beef 97
Creole Mustard Beef Oscar 98
Easy Asian Steak 99
English Pub-Style Beef 100
Fantastic Beef Fajitas 101
Fettucine with Roasted Red Pepper & Garlic Cream
      Sauce 102
Flaming Fajitas 103
Greek Steak Sandwich 55
Grilled Beef Tenderloin with Goat Cheese 104
Involtini of Sirloin Steak 105
Java Pepper Steak 106
Key Lime Steaks 107
Lemon Pepper Steak For Two 108
Louis' Cola-Kiwi Steaks 109
Low-Fat Honey Dijon Marinated Steak 110
Mandarin Orange Pepper Steak 111
Middle Eastern Grilled Steak Pockets 112
Moroccan Beef with Tabbouleh 113
Mustard Medallions with Sage Onion Compote 114
Orange Ginger Beef Stir-Fry 115
Original Swiss Steak 116
Peppered Steaks with Caramelized Onions & Fruit
      Salsa 117
Pizza-Style Minute Steaks 59
Pizza with Pastrami-Spiced Beef 118
Port Glazed Steak with Poached Pears & Blue
      Cheese 119
Prairie-Style Tri-Tip Steaks 120
Raclette-Style Beef in Herbed Butter 121
Ranch-Style Beef Kabobs & Rice 122
Sesame Ginger Beef Stir-Fry 61
Spanish Fiesta Steak 123
Steak and Pepper Heroes 62
Steak and Smoked Salmon Roll 124
Steak Diane 125
Strip Loins in Wine Sauce 126
T-Bone Steaks with Pistou 127
Thai Beef Satay 63
Thai Beef Stir-Fry 128
Thai Spicy Beef with Noodles 64
Two Tomato Beef Pasta 129
Weeknight Steak Dinner 130
Steak and Pepper Heroes 62
Steak and Smoked Salmon Roll 124

Steak Diane 125
Stewing Beef
   Beef & Portobello Stew 131
   Beef Bourguignon 132
   Country Beef Ragout 134
   Curried Beef Stew 135
   Homestyle Beef Stew 136
   Maple-Glazed Beef 137
   Pastry-Topped Ginger Beef 138
   Simple Beef Goulash 139
   Traditional Braised Beef Stew 140
Stir-Fry
   Hawaiian Beef Stir-Fry 57
   Mediterranean Beef Stir-Fry 58
   Sesame Ginger Beef Stir-Fry 61
   Thai Beef Stir-Fry 128
Strip Loins in Wine Sauce 126
Stuffed Cranberry Roast 84
Surf & Turf Beef Roast 85

T-Bone Steaks with Pistou 127
Tangy Oktoberfest Roast 86
Tangy Thai Beef Pinwheels 32
Teriyaki Surf & Turf Salad 33
Tex-Mex Ribs 87
Thai Beef Satay 63
Thai Beef Stir-Fry 128
Thai Beef Wraps 34
Thai Spicy Beef with Noodles 64
Traditional Braised Beef Stew 140
Two Tomato Beef Pasta 129

Vietnamese Soup 35

Warm Beef & Berry Salad 36
Weeknight Steak Dinner 130